PASSIONATE AND PROFITABLE

PASSIONATE AND PROFITABLE

WHY CUSTOMER STRATEGIES FAIL
AND TEN STEPS TO DO THEM RIGHT

LIOR ARUSSY

JOHN WILEY & SONS, INC.

Published by John Wiley & Sons, Inc., Hoboken, New Jersey.
Published simultaneously in Canada.

Library of Congress Cataloging-in-Publication Data:

Arussy, Lior.
  Passionate and profitable : why customer strategies fail and ten steps to do them right / Lior Arussy.
    p. cm.
  Includes bibliographical references and index.
    ISBN 0-471-71392-9 (cloth)
    1. Customer services—Management. 2. Customer relations. 3. Strategic planning.
  4. Consumer satisfaction. I. Title.
  HF5415.5.A784 2005
  658.8'02—dc22   2004022230

Printed in the United States of America

10 9 8 7 6 5 4 3 2 1

To All My Clients for Being
My Best Teachers

ACKNOWLEDGMENTS

Throughout my work experience, I came across many cases of both success and failure. It is to the hundreds of clients who had the courage and willingness to share their experiences that we owe gratitude and appreciation. They are too many to name, but their contribution, nevertheless, was significant. And as such it is to them that this book is dedicated.

Special thanks to Bill Wear for being a trusted advisor, an honest editor, and simply a friend. Thanks to the team at Wiley, Jackie Smith, Sheck Cho, Colleen Scollans, Rose Sullivan, Natasha Andrews, Petrina Kulek, and Diana Hawthorne, for bringing this book to life—I could not have done that without you.

To my family who keeps on accepting and supporting my passion, there are no words to describe my gratitude to you. I love you. Thank God.

CONTENTS

INTRODUCTION:
THE TOP TEN CRUCIAL MISTAKES IN CUSTOMER STRATEGIES

Succeeding in business is a straightforward matter: focus on the customers and amaze them with experiences that exceed their expectations. They will respond with repeat business and longer loyalty.

This would seem to be a simple, common-sense guideline; nevertheless, it appears to be more difficult than ever to convince customers to be loyal and deliver greater business.

The reason is that we don't always *do* what we *know,* or do not know how to do what we want. After years of research and consulting, I discovered that most companies don't really know *how* to do what they *think* they know. "We are committed to our customers" or "Customers are the reason for our existence" are common slogans hanging on many corporate walls. But what does it mean from an operational viewpoint? How do we put these lofty statements into practice?

Many organizations say "the customer is king"—but do we really love customers and strive to delight them? Or are they merely a way to make money? Are we passionately obsessed with making people happy every day, or are customers the burden we bear because we weren't born rich or didn't win the lottery? Ask yourself: if you had all the money you needed and then some, would you still be energized every day by a mission to help people solve their problems?

This book is about making the choice for the customer, making a choice beyond the superficial slogans and choosing an operational, actionable strategy. Our experience has shown that although companies focus their customer programs on cross-selling and loyalty initiatives, the issue is much more fundamental. They fail in their value proposition—their total customer experience. One of the critical rules discussed in this book is: *whoever collects and completes the value proposition gets to keep most of the money.* A few companies deliver a complete, clear, and compelling value proposition to their customers, so they collect premium prices. However, most companies leave their customers to unravel the value of products and services on their own, so they reap a poor return. The real money—in any game—is not in the old four "Ps": Product, Pricing, Placement, and Promotion. The glitz and glamour of the product does not *really* cause people to beat a path to your door; you can build it, but this doesn't mean customers will come wandering out of the cornfield to plunk down $20 for it. In fact, product differentiation evaporates faster than ever because of private-label alternatives. The attractiveness of the price doesn't get customers either and is easily compromised through Web retailers who compete on the basis of the lowest price ever. Nor will a fancy display in a high-traffic channel bring them, and promotions are a dime a dozen. Many alternatives are available to your customers, alternatives that will challenge your premium placement. If you want to win loyalty and create a customer base with an almost fanatical devotion to your products, you need to create a complete experience, an amazing and surprising experience, that is, a value proposition.

This book will detail the critical decisions and trade-offs companies must make to focus their efforts on the customer. To live and breathe the customers, just as your company used to do when it was founded by a passionate entrepreneur, requires that you make strategic choices. These tough but necessary choices are what this book is about. In fact, the book will argue that these choices are at the core of customer relationships: companies that do not commit to customer relationships do not keep customers; companies that do can hardly keep up with demand. These commitments cannot be faked or subjected to quarterly demands. They are long term by nature.

Before we discuss the choices, let's review the state of the industry and the fatal mistakes that companies make every day in their customer relationships.

THE GRAVEYARD OF GOOD INTENTIONS

Let's start by stating what companies are definitely *not* lacking. Companies do not lack intention or initiative. Throughout the corporate world, customer-related activities have been undertaken as "initiatives," "programs," or "campaigns"; they run for a short period but are never embraced as a full operational strategy. The customer mantra has been placed at the top of the list in memos and corporate declarations and has been incorporated into myriad T-shirts, giveaways, and posters plastered all over company headquarters. Companies also do not lack great slogans. From "going the extra mile" to "total customer commitment," companies detail their intentions in manuals, brochures, and advertising. Companies have wanted to believe that they could drip a little customer sauce over their self-centered organizations and call it done. Guess what? It isn't working.

Intentions and initiatives are many, but sustainable success is rare. Great slogans are a dime a dozen. The harder task is to live the slogans and execute them when one is forced to choose between efficiency and customer loyalty. For most companies, it seems that intention and short-term initiatives are the peak of success.

This problem is reflected in corporate budgets. Significant effort and resources are allocated to customer focus, but long-term results are few. For decades, companies have chanted the mantra that they listen to customers and produce what customers want. Business books, gurus, and university professors have preached these messages for years. On any given Saturday, nearly every golf course in the country has four or five conversations going on that end with, "All you have to do is give the customers what they want!" I don't know of a single company that doesn't claim to put the customer first. And yet, despite all the bragging, very few companies can demonstrate long-term success in forming strong, sustainable, and profitable customer relationships. Why should it be so difficult to pull off something that is, in principle, so simple? These questions are at the core of every corporation's customer challenge.

The pursuit of a customer is a decades-long exercise to which every company claims complete commitment, and yet customer relationships and loyalty are in constant decline. Even after several years of multibillion-dollar customer relationship programs and other customer initiatives, very few companies have forged lasting relationships. Of course, very few companies actually have *effective* customer relationship programs: information is collected, but not combined, stored, managed, or analyzed for the purposes of drawing conclusions or classifying customers. As a result, companies usually don't know their customers. What happens if you want to update a product: do you even know who is using the old versions? Do you know which customers have quit using your products but are still paying for support simply because it's easier and less confrontational to pass along a small monthly fee so you won't bother them again for a couple of years?

There is an interesting hint here: customer programs were wanted and conceived but not implemented correctly or completely, so they are not working well. According to the Gartner Group, only 50% of the current customer programs will be considered a success by 2007. This is an unacceptable success rate that in any other circumstances would have kept companies from implementing a program. The Strativity Group's study[1] demonstrated that 45% of executives surveyed do not believe they deserve the customer's loyalty. Why is it that so many companies fail in what should be their number-one task? How it is possible that billions of dollars later, companies still show such poor results in gaining and retaining customers? Why is it that despite all the investment, companies fail to attract and retain customers' hearts (and, of course, a portion of their budgets)? What are the reasons that—despite all the demonstrations of affection—we do not seem to be able to make our targets fall in love with our products, services, and companies?

"I will kiss you for exactly three seconds,
at precisely 2 o'clock sharp."

Many companies have focused on a self-serving, efficient, transactional approach, as opposed to the generous, long-term nurturing required for a real relationship. If customers were from Venus, to quote the popular book, companies were living on Mars (or even Pluto!), seeking a quick return with minimal investment and attachment. These companies did not make the important choices necessary to forge a real, long-term relationship, which requires change and adaptation. (Note: this does *not* imply the incremental quality approach of continuous improvement.) Even now, such companies are trying to keep their own efficiency-based identities and seeking customer relationships on their terms. Like self-centered bachelors, they want to believe that a few superficial acts will substitute for what is required to form a true, lasting relationship.

One of the best examples of efficiency gone awry is the organizational chart. Many companies are functionally organized on the basis of expertise, rather than on value to customers. Thus each functional area specializes in only one aspect of the business, and the other aspects are ignored. Employees focus on their well-defined areas of responsibility, drawn from procedure and process, forcing the customer to become subservient to company policy. "I am responsible for the left nostril; anything else is someone else's job," they say, or "My job is to focus on the upper part of the right ears; the rest is not my job." The expertise-based organizational chart creates silos, when each function protects its own turf and agenda, leaving the customer to collect the pieces and assemble the total value proposition.

The organizational chart is also a prime example of another factor that limits customer focus: indecisiveness. Today's pathetic results in instituting customer strategies can be attributed to *inability* to make the required tough decisions, *reluctance* to make the tough decisions, or *just plain indecisiveness.* Corporations have failed to address the key issues and make a set of hard decisions (which are the focus of this book); they have therefore failed to change their organization. This means that good intentions are never translated into operational excellence. In our research and consulting engagements, we have observed these telltale signs again and again: multiple symptoms indicating the lack of meaningful customer strategy choices.

Indecisiveness turns out to be worse than a lack of decisions. No decision does *not* equal no action. In most cases, it leads the company back to old, self-centered ways of doing business.What is even worse, neglecting to decide on just one or two key issues will often damage other decisions and lead the entire strategy to failure.

There are two subtle but deadly forms of indecisiveness that plague customer initiatives. The first is conflicting decisions: while a certain decision is being implemented, a conflicting one will be made, lessening the impact of the customer-related choice. This lack of consistency is a common pattern in customer strategies, as companies struggle to achieve greater profitability and efficiency.

The second deadly "decision sin" is myopia—plain old nearsightedness. Although a good customer strategy decision is made, a few months later the decision is reversed by a totally unrelated initiative, well ahead of its payoff. Thus the well-planned strategy disappears, and the organization focuses on newly defined, customer-irrelevant goals.

Making the choice to court customers is not just about a decision, it's a lifestyle change. Diets alone don't work and neither do solitary decisions. For a choice or strategy to be effective, it must be diffused throughout the organization, implemented for the long haul, and accompanied by the required changes to adapt to customer expectations. The choice is really about execution, not declarations. Like personal life, the customer is judging you by what you do, not by what you say. Making the choice to adapt and change is necessary for a relationship that goes beyond the occasional and accidental.

FAILURE FACTORS

In following success and failure cases around the world, as well as working with our clients, our experience and research points out multiple failure factors that are standing between companies and their customers. We often find that a company's failure results from the combination of several factors. These *failure factors,* which we will discuss in Chapter 1, are equally relevant for business-to-business companies and business-to-consumer companies. In this book we give many examples of companies that made the right customer choices, as well as some that did not. The companies described did not necessarily make *all* the right choices, but in the choices they *did* make, we found lessons to be shared with others and guidance for those who are seeking to make the right customer choices.

To enrich your personal experience, this book includes exercises that will allow you to apply these principles to your own business. Since the book is intended not only to challenge you but also to assist you to move toward action, the exercises were designed to help you apply your learning to the specific market and business conditions you face every day. Thus you can begin to build your own action plan—making the right choices and avoiding the fatal mistakes.

This book may not be an easy journey, but those who are committed to embracing challenge and making the right choices will win the rewards. The rewards will come in the form of the four new Ps, which are based on *actions* that will benefit the customer, not on perceptions: Premium price, Preference, Portion of budget, and Permanence of relationships. These are the rewards that customers will give the vendors who make the right choice to forge a sincere and lasting relationship.

This book is about helping you make the right customer choices; let the journey begin.

Endnote

1. Strativity, CEM 2003 Annual Global Study by Strativity Group, Livingston, NJ.

1

UNDERSTANDING THE FATAL MISTAKES

The pursuit of the customer is as old as the search for business success, and we have yet to see a company that will not declare total, undeniable dedication to the customer. Every company believes that they are focused on customers. They have a long list of initiatives to prove it. At the same time, customers feel more neglected than ever. Customer frustration is sky-rocketing, and very few companies can demonstrate long, sustainable, and profitable relationships with their customers.

Considerable attention has been focused on customers in the last decade, as shown by certain investments and declared commitments. It is well understood that without a loyal customer, no business can exist. Customers ought to be the center of everything we do. We ought to love, hug, delight, and please customers every day, with everything we do. Why is it then that despite great intentions, companies manage to fail in the most important task they have: attracting and retaining customers? Why is it that despite billions of dollars in investment, executives have very little to show in the form of results?

There is no single answer to this question. In our consulting and research work, we have come across many reasons for failure. We call them the *Fatal Mistakes*. For many companies, the answer is a combination of several Fatal Mistakes.

The Fatal Mistakes are considered fatal because companies fail to notice them and to understand how significant they are to customer success. For many organizations, the existence of the Fatal Mistakes means that even before a customer initiative is launched, failure is ensured. They are fatal because they are woven into corporate behavior and culture. They have become an integral part of the corporate DNA and thus are difficult to remove. Companies often try to launch customer programs, knowing about these Fatal Mistakes but wanting to believe that such programs will work anyway. This is just wishful thinking.

1

Unless companies address and uproot these Fatal Mistakes, their customer initiatives will continue to fail, despite the money invested and the level of commitment demonstrated. Customer-centric strategy cannot coexist with these Fatal Mistakes. As with most strategies, it boils down to a trade-off between tough choices. Ignoring these Fatal Mistakes is a choice companies make every day, one that works against the customer.

FATAL MISTAKE 1: CULTURE OF THE NEW

Companies admire and adore new things: new products, new customers, new deals, new territories. We live in a culture in which new is admired and old is rejected. Maintenance of the existing is drudgery, left to the lower paid, least important employees; trail-blazing of the new is the privilege of bright, talented executives. Compensation is traditionally higher for new customer acquisitions than for sales to existing customers. This cultural phenomenon sends a clear message about what is appreciated and rewarded in the organization—and therefore where resources should be invested. Employees, taking their cue from top management, will emulate the "new" culture in everyday work. In an environment of ever more limited resources, in which fewer projects get attention, the culture of the new will lead employees to neglect the care and maintenance of existing customers.

In this culture, maintaining and nurturing existing customers is regarded as secondary. We love to sell to one customer and move on to the next. Customers quickly get the message that the honeymoon is over, their business is being taken for granted, and they will no longer command priority attention. Adapting the company's lesson to their own situation, customers seek new vendors who will treat them as new customers.

FATAL MISTAKE 2: LIPSTICK ON THE PIG

For many companies, the customer strategy is not an in-depth change of processes, behavior, and methods. It is common for companies to assume that their rather tight and highly efficient operation (which hardly regards customer needs) can stay intact with no changes. On top of that concept, they create a new frosting to decorate their company with a customer-friendly face. These companies treat customer strategies as cosmetics, with colorful commercials, ads, and brochures promising increased commitment and heightening expectations. The customer strategy is not an in-depth change in processes, behavior, and methods. Such companies never bother to examine what needs to change internally, in areas such as products and operations, to complement and fulfill those promises. In fact, most companies hope they will not need to change anything *but* the external appearance. They want to believe that the lipstick will hide the pig and make it look like a swan.

After years of broken promises, customers are well trained in detecting a pig from a distance, regardless of how much lipstick it wears. Worse yet, the companies themselves have trained customers to be suspicious and cynical and to reject upfront any attempt to cover up the truth with cosmetics.

FATAL MISTAKE 3: PASSION LOSS

In the beginning, there was an entrepreneur with a noble idea to make life better through a new product or service. This entrepreneur used passion to create and sell new products. In fact, the company was running on passion—which was contagious and caught customer attention. This passion also drove the company to understand customers better (as well as the reasons they purchase products). Then the company grew, and the bean counters took over. They processed everything and stripped away the most important intangible asset: passion. Without a passion for customers, no strategy will work.

Products and customers are two separate entities, which require glue or chemistry to connect them. Without this chemistry, the product is just another set of capabilities. It is actually not the products or services but the way they interact with customers that creates the appeal and the drive to purchase. For many young companies, the passion provides the glue—a personal touch that makes the product or service appealing. Without this passion, the product becomes undifferentiated and similar to competitive offerings. It loses the chemistry that makes it desirable. Companies will repeatedly deny that they have lost passion when in fact they have, and in the process they have lost the bond with the customer. Loss of passion means losing the core reason for being in business and often equates to sinking into the abyss of commoditization in the name of cost control.

FATAL MISTAKE 4: REAL COST OF COST REDUCTION

Companies that focus on cost cutting must confront a simple truth that they prefer to ignore or deny: there is no such thing as a free cost reduction program. Any balance sheet will tell you that if you take from one side of the equation, you affect the other side—a simple rule that every bean counter knows well. However, the unasked question in a cost reduction program is: Who pays the price?

Customers pay the price. Cost cutting leads to accelerated commoditization of products and services. Customers begin to see fewer unique and differentiated products. Cost reduction also means fewer people to serve customers, so more of the service is done by the customers themselves. The people who stay on board to serve customers are not as excited and ambitious because their morale is so low. Cost reduction exacts an enormous price, and the prime target is our usual victim—the customer.

As organizations rush to brag to investors about successful cost reduction programs, they neglect to disclose the real price. They act as if cost reduction affects nothing and no one, as if it is possible to cut costs without doing any damage. In reality, cost-cutting efforts over the last few years have significantly diluted relationships with customers. As companies face the challenge of growth, they are also facing disgruntled customers who are resentful that *they* were left to bear the consequences. Chances are slim that customers will offer loyalty or long-term commitment after such experiences.

FATAL MISTAKE 5: FAILURE TO OPERATIONALIZE

What does it mean to implement a customer strategy? How does it impact on the shipping department or accounts receivable? An operational plan is frequently missing. How do we change and align a company around the customer? What changes are even required? Most of the available experience and research focuses on the starting point of the process, perhaps on designing some new messaging or positioning, but very little is done in the form of a full operational plan to implement an organization-wide customer strategy.

Lack of an operational plan means that strategy objectives are not fully disseminated in company policy or employee behavior. As a result, the organization does not live its strategy, but rather treats it as a nice poster on the wall—a mission statement meant to inspire but not to be executed.

FATAL MISTAKE 6: YOU GET WHAT YOU PAY FOR

Current compensation plans focus on productivity. Maybe the rewards come in the form of lead generation incentives for the marketing department, quotas for the sales force, or production quantity for the operations depart-ment. Either way, the focus is on quantity and not quality. This is the current modus operandi, and this is how employees align themselves. You cannot continue to pay people on the basis of productivity alone and expect vol-untary focus on quality of service—it simply will not work.

Any major strategic change does not exist if it does not impact on people's performance evaluation and compensation package. Changes to compensation plans are usually harder to implement, so companies prefer to disregard them, hoping they will get away with superficial rewards. In reality, by ignoring these critical changes, they signal to their employees that customer strategies are *not* strategic. Employees perceive these infor-mal cues and prioritize their work accordingly. When employers choose to bypass customer-related compensation changes, they send a clear mes-sage: "This is not important to us, but we want you to volunteer to take care of this yourself." A few top-notch employees may spend some time on cus-tomers as a way to get ahead, but "Ignore this Matter" is the conclusion most employees draw when compensation does not encourage customer-focused behavior. After all, if it is not important enough for the paycheck, it must not be very important to the company.

FATAL MISTAKE 7: MANAGEMENT OF CHANGE

Change does not happen by itself. Customer strategies require some funda-mental internal changes. For companies that spent years organized around products or operational efficiency, customer strategies require major changes, ranging from updated roles and responsibilities to completely new organi-zational charts. People react differently to change, but most of them are fear-ful of its implications, often perceiving change as a personal threat. Just because a CEO's memo lands in the inbox, it does not mean people rush to execute its direction.

Often we see deliberate or unconscious behavior geared toward top-pling customer efforts. This behavior is often motivated *by* fear of change, blinding employees to the reasons and benefits of customer programs and focusing on negatives they may experience. Change management must be embedded in the strategy, along with a healthy dose of employee and manager training. Employees need to be sold on the initiative, and proper change management analysis must be incorporated into the strategy to mobilize change within the organization. A memo from the CEO will not cut it.

FATAL MISTAKE 8: LACK OF LEADERSHIP

When you look into CEO suites these days, you find many veterans of finance or operations but very few with a background in marketing, sales, or human relations. Corporate leaders are experts in efficiency and number crunching but are not well versed in human aspects. After several decades of experience, such executives tend to view the world through the lens that makes them most comfortable, the same perspective that got them to the top job. Like most people, they simply stay in their comfort zone.

Customer strategies require leadership that sees the business from the customer's view, not through a spreadsheet. Such strategies require leaders with people skills and a sincere appreciation of human assets. The odds are against finance or operations specialists, trained for years in the art of number crunching, as they try to rise to the challenge. They are not to be blamed, because years of habit cannot be erased—but it does not change the fact that true leaders who "get it" are missing in the ranks of upper management.

FATAL MISTAKE 9: UNSTRUCTURED RELATIONSHIP

Most customer relationships are not structured to continue beyond the initial sale. It's often the case that we have nothing else to sell. Needless to say, this approach is costly, because the total sales revenues compared with the cost of courting new customers makes it highly expensive way to do business. Companies do not structure their relationships with customers for the long run. They treat their customers as a destination and not a journey. Every sale is a one-time accomplishment, instead of a long-term commitment.

In our research, we could not find a single well-documented customer plan detailing a two- to three-year relationship—let alone a ten-year plan—with multiple purchases and further commitments. We found many empty slogans, but no documented plans. Companies often leave that part to luck. Trained to acquire customers, they often puzzle over what to do with them beyond the initial sale. It is always amazing how such a crucial part of the business is left to vague, incidental outcomes and not developed as a well-planned and carefully executed strategy.

Lack of structured relationships means confusion and inaction. Without a structured customer relationship, companies often default to the bad behavior of chasing new customers and establishing too many short-lived relationships. By doing so, we leave our customers exposed to the assault of our competition.

Structuring relationships is about responding to expectations and ensuring longevity, which leads to greater revenues per customer and higher profitability. Unfortunately, despite the common-sense justifications, most organizations are operating on a whim and not a well-structured relationship plan.

FATAL MISTAKE 10: TECHNOLOGY SHORTCUT

For many companies, customer strategy development means buying a piece of technology. They want to believe that a magic gizmo will relieve them of the need to confront the tough tasks of strategic planning, process development, and change management. Technology is merely a tool. It cannot do the job for you. You cannot simply buy a hammer and a saw and expect a full dining room set to happen by itself. No brush and collection of paints will create a masterpiece. In fact, it's foolish to buy tools at all before you have a plan dictating which ones you need. After all, what colors should you buy for your masterpiece if you do not know what you are going to paint? Common-sense logic does not stop many companies from attempting to take the technology shortcut.

The temptation that this shortcut might work is often too sweet to pass up. Needless to say, like most other shortcuts, technology delivers only short-term benefits and, in the worst case, damages customer relationships. As in real life, there are no shortcuts when it comes to people. Deeper relationships with customers, like deeper relationships with loved ones, cannot exist in a shortcut environment.

If companies truly seek profitable, lasting relationships, they will have to make a series of tough decisions to determine their success. The first decision is to stop the indecision. The lack of an active decision to address the Fatal Mistakes is a form of choice—a choice that prefers the current operational mode over a customer-centric strategy. By not making the decision to eliminate the root cause of the problem, the fatal failure, companies vote against their customers.

To achieve a customer-centric business model, companies ought to address the Fatal Mistakes first. They ought to eliminate such mistakes from their operation in order to start following the proposed choices that will put them on the path to customer focus. The ability to address these tough choices and all related issues will directly control whether they continue to stagnate or shift toward customer-centric thinking as a way of doing business. Anything else usually overpromises and underdelivers and is bound to fail: in the absence of decisions, companies will default to the Fatal Mistakes.

Yes, choosing to focus on customers is not a simple, overnight change to the corporate slide deck. It has multiple implications and impacts, from the way the company designs products and services to the way it compensates people, to the length of the product life cycle and the next innovation. Companies will have to make complex decisions and measured trade-offs, asking questions such as:

- What is the role of the customer in the organization—a means to an end or the ultimate end?
- What is the company's chief priority: efficiency or customers?
- Are we conducting a true dialogue with customers or merely paying lip service to ideas we don't grasp?

All these choices—and many more—build the blueprint toward truly sustainable, profitable customer strategies. Making a few wrong decisions along the way weakens the strategy and its implementation, undermining the best intentions and the most valiant efforts.

CRITICAL CHOICES

The critical choices are the choices every company must face in order to decide if it is ready to become customer focused. These are not choices in the sense that you either do them or not. This is exactly the mistake many companies have made. If you decide to become customer focused, you must make these choices. They are not optional. Some companies made some of these choices. But rarely did a company cover all the choices. The critical choices listed below will be discussed in the following chapters. Each chapter will be dedicated to a choice and will explain the full scope of the choice and the right way to make it.

- What is the role of the customer in our existence: a means to an end or the endgame?
- Which customers do we neglect? Are we taking every customer willing to pay?
- What defines our total experience? Are we a silo function focused organization, with each function owning a piece of the customer, or are we a complete, holistic customer organization? What kind of relationships do we seek? Are we in the self-serving, efficient, transaction realm, or do we seek a generous, long-term relationship?
- How do we change ourselves to avoid the silo-based customer trap? How do we assume complete customer responsibility?

- Do we employ functional robots or passionate evangelists? What people should we employ to deliver the best customer experience?
- On the question of dialogue and feedback, do we really care? Do we have the willingness and mechanism to listen?
- What do our measurements say about us? Do we encourage playing by the rules or breaking them?
- How long do we milk our products? Is innovation the exception or the rule?

The ultimate commitment—a deep, customer-focused strategy—is a mutual, lifetime commitment.

In the long history of pursuing the customer, some companies have actively made some of these choices, but very few have made them all. Addressing some of these decisions and ignoring the rest is equivalent to being on a diet only between 5 and 9 in the morning and then allowing yourself to go wild with your eating in the rest of the day. Only complete commitment can deliver the desired results. Only complete commitment to eliminating the Fatal Mistakes and actively making the complete series of customer choices can result in a successful customer strategy. Customers will deliver their full financial and emotional commitment only to those companies that will reciprocate. Trying to compromise on the commitment will result in a similar response from the customer. There is no such thing as 35% loyalty; it is either 100% loyalty or none at all. This is how the customer is watching your company's choices and actions. Customer loyalty and long-term commitment will be earned by companies that make 100% commitment and do not attempt to compromise.

The next few chapters detail the required commitments as expected and perceived by the customer. When companies wear customer lenses and assume the customer's perspective, they will be able to start making the right choices.

2

CRITICAL CHOICE 1:
WHO ARE WE, CUSTOMER PLEASERS
OR EFFICIENCY CRUNCHERS?

Customers—do we really love them and strive to delight them? Or do they constitute a way to make money because we couldn't come up with a better idea to pay for our needs? Are we passionately obsessed with making people happy and making them smile every day? Or are customers the burden we must bear because we weren't born rich or we didn't win the lottery? Are customers the end goal or the means for a completely different goal? The answer to this question will determine your level of commitment to the customer. As an end goal, your commitment to the customer is high and absolute. When the customer is a means to an end, you only do the bare necessities.

These questions are at the core of the customer–corporation challenge. The choices they present will lead every step of your operation, dictate every aspect of employee behavior, and help you reach overall success in your customer strategy. Neglecting to address these questions will default you to self-serving behavior that alienates your customers and puts your sales and margins on a downward spiral.

After several years of multibillion-dollar investments in customer relationship management programs and other customer initiatives, very few companies have managed to forge lasting relationships with their customers. Despite an average 20% growth in investment in customer service centers, customers still regard telephone service representatives as one of the most hated facets of the corporation. In an article in *Newsweek* magazine, Jonathan Alter[1] argued that the average customer service representative can take a healthy person and transform him or her into a candidate for coronary surgery in less than 60 seconds. Unfortunately, most customers agree.

Why is it that so many smart executives cannot get customer relationships right in the first place? Unlike other corporate tasks, this one should be easier, considering that every executive is also a customer. If you are like most executives, you regard yourself as customer focused. You have the T-shirts and posters to prove it, including—of course—your memos and your own collection of customer-related books. Well, let's examine a simple question: how many of your customers receive a birthday card from you? Let's try another one: how many customer birthdays do you actually know? What do you think will happen if you forget to buy a birthday card for your loved one? How well do you think your relationships will flourish if you tell people you do not even remember their birthdays? When one applies personal experience to the customer-centric issue in the business world, an interesting perspective is revealed. This application is not for illustration purposes only; it is quite relevant and goes to the core of customer relationships. Customers are emotional by nature, not just logical. Treating them as a set of financial transactions and ignoring their emotional side misses the whole point of relationships.

The source of the problem in customer–company relationships was the focus of our most recent global study.[2] Unlike the approach of other studies, we did not ask the customers to tell us what's wrong, as many have already done. This time we approached the executives at leading companies around the world. We surveyed 165 customer service and marketing executives from North America, Europe, Asia, and Africa, asking them about the customer-related issues and customer commitment. These executives were drawn from both Fortune 2000 and emerging companies. Responses were charted with respect to creating and delivering value to customers—the exact value proposition that is supposed to command relationships and loyalty. We wanted to hear from the inside what is really going on. This year-long study, which included face-to-face interactions, revealed some fundamental issues that expose the truth behind customer–corporation relationships. These are among our findings:

- A total of 60% claimed that their relationships with the customer are not well defined or structured.
- A total of 42% claimed that their company takes any customer who is willing to pay; in Business-to-Business (B2B) and services businesses the numbers are 72% and 69%, respectively.
- A total of 46% claimed that their executives are not meeting with customers frequently.
- Only 32% claimed that their compensation is tied to quality of service.
- Only 37% agreed that they have the tools to address and resolve customer problems.

- Only 36% agreed that their company invests in people more than in technology (38% in the United States and 10% in Europe).
- Only 36% of European respondents agreed that their company deserves the customer's loyalty versus 54% of the American respondents.

LACK OF DEFINITION AND CRITERIA

The above results demonstrate that there are fundamental flaws in relationships between customers and corporations. Corporations are hardly addressing the issue of developing a well-defined and structured relationship with a customer with clear expectations on both sides. Whereas 41% of the U.S. respondents agreed that the role of the customer is well defined, only 17% of their European counterparts agreed with that statement. When we requested examples from those who claimed to have well-defined relationships, the responses failed to address the issue properly and completely. This finding represents a lack of full understanding of what companies are seeking from their relationships with customers. When respondents were confronted with questions such as "how long does the company seek to have a relationship" and "with what level of margins," the percent that was able to answer those questions was in the single-digit range. With such unclear focus, it is impossible to forge long-term commitments, let alone maximize opportunities or deliver full value to customers. This state of vagueness also results in an inability to plan the relationship for the long term and build success milestones along the way. The result is an attitude that treats customers as a one-time acquisition and then rushes to pursue the next one, leaving the newly acquired customers wondering if they made the right choice.

More than 41% of the respondents agreed that their company takes any customer willing to pay. When the results were segmented by industry, it was surprising to discover that in relationship-intensive industries such as business-to-business companies, the number jumped to 52%. These figures represent a lack of basic selection of customers who are suitable and capable of appreciating the company's proposed experience. Lack of basic customer selection leads to relationships with the wrong customers—those who will later become unprofitable. Many companies suffer from an inability to select customers who appreciate the value proposition and are willing to pay premium prices for it. The result is wasted resources applied to customers who are inherently unsuitable to be in a relationship with your company. This approach represents a strong *product* rather than *customer* focus, an attitude of "if they know how to spell our name and have a budget, they are a target customer."

Exhibit 2.1   Company Is Willing to Take Any Customer Willing to Pay, by Industry Segments

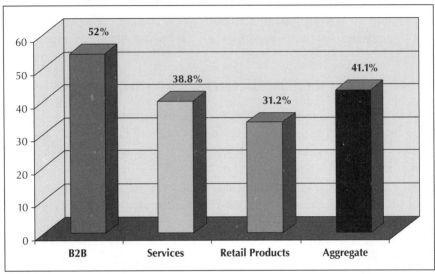

As we can see in Exhibit 2.1, overall, 41.1% of the respondents claimed that they take every customer willing to pay regardless of suitability to the customer relationship structure. A surprising finding was to see the results in the B2B sector jump to 52%. For a business sector that is highly dependent on relationships and should have sufficient time to qualify customers, the desperation for business, any business, is high. As a result, companies are diluting their customer base with unsuitable customers who will cost them in the long run in the form of high maintenance expenses and loss of qualified customers. Qualified customers, having to compete with unsuitable customers for limited company service resources, will eventually give up and defect to competitors. Serving unsuitable customers means fewer resources, hence less satisfaction to the qualified customers.

INTENTION TO EXECUTION GAP

Employee experiences emerged as another alarming issue (Exhibit 2.2). Although a surprising 73.4% of respondents agreed that their employer deserved their loyalty, when respondents were asked about specific actions, the agreement level dropped:

- Only 37% agreed that their company invests in people more than technology.

- Only 37.2% agreed that they have the tools and authority to solve customer problems.

- Only 33% agreed that the compensation plan emphasizes quality over productivity.

These results are alarming, especially because they are coming from executives and not lower level employees. If the general conviction among two-thirds of the leaders is that they do not have the tools, authority, or investment to service customers, they will act accordingly. And, regardless of declarations, the troops will follow the leaders' actions. Lacking conviction, they are not likely to lead their organization into service excellence or well-differentiated products.

In an era of ever increasing commoditization of products and services, companies are increasingly more dependent on their service personnel to create differentiating, commanding, premium experiences. When customers can hardly see the difference between competing products and services, the human services step in to create the desired differentiation. It is the people and the way they deliver the products and services that justify the premium price or the preference. Customers associate greater value with service (and the complete experience around the products) than with the value provided by the products themselves. The above results indicate that companies fail to understand these factors and to give customers a total experience accordingly.

Exhibit 2.2   Respondents Indicate Lack of Tools and Authority to Service Customers

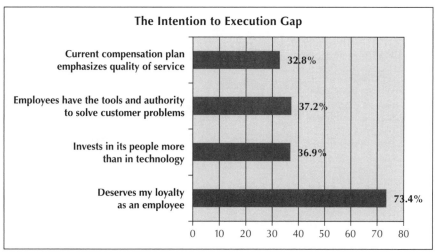

Although 58% of the surveyed executives agreed that their company is truly committed to the customer (61% in the United States and 46% in Europe; see Exhibit 2.3):

- 54.5% agreed that their company does not conduct a true dialogue with its customers.
- 53.8% agreed that their executives do not meet frequently with customers.
- 59.6% agreed that the role of the customer is not well defined.
- 44.6% agreed that their company does not deserve the customer's loyalty.
- 42% agreed that their company accepts any customer willing to pay.

These results indicate that many executives view their company's commitment to customers as largely superficial and nothing more than a revenue opportunity. Following the company's actions and not declarations, they are highly likely to perform accordingly. Despite all the promises made to customers about commitment to their satisfaction, the results demonstrate that most executives do not see those promises kept.

There are several issues that create difficulties for executives when marketing promises are translated into service and value realities.

PRICE OF EFFICIENCY

In the last few years, companies have adapted their marketing messages to claim complete commitment to customer success. Several movements

Exhibit 2.3   Data Demonstrating that Executives Hold a Superficial Commitment to a True Customer-Centric Culture

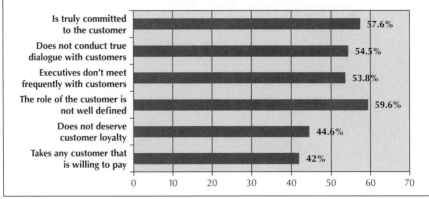

such as 1-to-1 marketing and customer relationship management have led organizations to expand their messages regarding the importance of customers. Their romantic advertising has created higher expectations among customers—expectations that were crushed the first time those customers contacted a customer service representative.

This saga did not start recently. Let's examine some interesting statements collected over the years:

*"In the 1960s we sold boxes, in the 1970s
we'll sell solutions to customer problems."*
—Ralph A. Pfeiffer, Head of IBM Data Processing Division, *Sales and
Marketing Management,* August 1972

*"We intend to change everything that needs changing in
our business in order to make ourselves as responsive as possible
to customer requirements."*
—C.B. Rogers Jr., Senior VP and group executive of IBM's Information
Systems Group, *Sales and Marketing Management,* January 1983

*"We're going to organize the sales force to give customers what
they want. We're going to start with the customer."*
—Louis V. Gerstner Jr., Chairman of IBM, *Sales and
Marketing Management,* July 1993

If these statements weren't so sad, they'd be funny—and this is not the case for IBM alone. Similar behavior can be tracked for almost any company. A company will declare commitment to customers and then fail to deliver. It seems that at least once a decade, the customer flag is raised again. Afterward, we somehow default to the traditional behavior of efficiency machines, focused on squeezing the system for every possible ounce of cost savings. We have just experienced the latest wave of cost cutting, as companies who could not demonstrate growth defaulted to cost reduction as a survival mode. It was also a way for executives to demonstrate "leadership" and fight for continued relevance. Millions of jobs were shed, and billions of dollars in cost savings were miraculously found. In their zeal to prove their importance, the cost-cutters forgot to report to Wall Street about the ultimate price and who pays it. The answer is quite simple: the customer.

The companies that focused on cost cutting also diluted the value of their products and services. The zeal to reduce costs led to accelerated commoditization of products. In response, customers became efficient as well, searching for the lowest prices and refusing to give their loyalty to a specific company. In the face of a bland product with no exciting features, the customer found no reason to pay a premium or to prefer one product over the other. Enter the price game.

As IBM was celebrating several billions of dollars in savings in 2003, I was wondering what products they might have commoditized even further, to the point that the customer would not have any reason to prefer them anymore. That is, until time for the next executive statement about customer commitment.

After Kraft Foods bought Stella D'Oro, a Bronx-based Italian bakery,[3] they decided to cut costs. The cost cutters identified waste in the old cookie recipe and decided to substitute lower cost dairy ingredients for the expensive, nondairy ingredients. In preparing for the change, the company relabeled its cookie packaging and indicated the dairy content. A drop in sales followed. Customers were not even trying the cookies marked as dairy. Deliverymen reported that cookie packages were left on the shelves for weeks, untouched. The once popular product had all of a sudden become an outcast. The reason was quite simple, but the cost cutters hadn't bothered to consider the market before their cost reduction decision. The nondairy cookies were very popular among orthodox Jews, who observe the separation of meat and dairy foods. Thus Stella D'Oro cookies were an integral part of their dietary regimen; they could enjoy the cookies while observing their religious laws. Lactose-intolerant people found the cookies appealing as well. They, too, could enjoy these great cookies without fear of a dairy ingredient that would endanger their health.

Kraft Foods eventually heard the voice of their customers and deliverymen and reversed their recipe decision. Many other companies use cost-cutting number-crunchers who do not measure the impact of their recommendations on the customer. Focusing on cost reduction and efficiency without investigating who is paying the real price is common, even at companies that declare their loyalty and commitment to customers.

The pendulum between customer focus and cost efficiency is constantly swinging, but somehow cost efficiency always wins.

The two natural sources of growth are customers and employees. Customers who are satisfied buy more at higher prices, are loyal for a longer time, and share the word with their friends and family. Employees who service the customers know whether or not they are creating differentiation through a unique and memorable experience, and this filters down to the employees who invent new products, services, and business models. This informal communication in turn affects the company's ability to ensure future revenues from customers who elect to stay with the company because of its high value and innovative products or services. Both customers and employees have been seriously affected by the last wave of cost cutting. The bond of trust has been severely eroded. Companies seeking growth are now facing a serious challenge. They will have to rebuild the trust factor before any growth will be possible.

Take the following aptitude test to examine the health of your relationship with your customers:

CORPORATION–CUSTOMER EXPERIENCE APTITUDE SURVEY

INSTRUCTIONS: Assume that the following statements represent your company's attitudes. Rate each statement from 1 (strongly disagree) to 5 (strongly agree). In assigning the values, consider both written company documents (i.e., mission, vision, values, etc.) and actual company behaviors.

1. The customer is a means to achieve our financial goals.   _____

2. Shareholder value is the reason for the company's existence.   _____

3. The customer is the heart of our business.   _____

4. The only way to win customer loyalty is to exceed their expectations.   _____

5. Earnings per share are at the highest level of importance in our company.   _____

6. The customer is always right.   _____

7. Not every customer is worth the investment.   _____

8. Our goal is to maximize our profits and minimize our expenses.   _____

9. An efficient operation is a successful operation.   _____

10. Shareholders run the show.   _____

11. Customers are the reason we are here.   _____

12. Customers are equal partners in the company.   _____

13. Customer satisfaction is the key to our success.   _____

14. Our customers are our number-one asset.   _____

15. Good processes are the way to achieve excellence.   _____

16. Customer satisfaction is dependent on employee satisfaction.   _____

17. Market-share is important to our success.   _____

18. Our customers' names/logos decorate our walls.   _____

19. We compensate employees primarily based on productivity.   _____

20. We are the market leader.   _____

21. Customer thank-you letters are frequently received.   _____

22. We are a global player.   _____

23. Everyone knows who the "star" servicepeople are.   _____

24. We are market driven.   _____

25. In our call center, the goal is to get callers off the line.   _____

Scoring

INSTRUCTIONS: For the number of each question listed below, circle the rating you gave it in the column directly below it. Then draw a line connecting all the circled answers.

25	9	17	2	19	22	20	1	5	8	10	15	13	14	11	6	23	3	4	7	12	16	24	21	18
5	5	5	5	5	5	5	5	5	5	5	5	5	5	5	5	5	5	5	5	5	5	5	5	5
4	4	4	4	4	4	4	4	4	4	4	4	4	4	4	4	4	4	4	4	4	4	4	4	4
3	3	3	3	3	3	3	3	3	3	3	3	3	3	3	3	3	3	3	3	3	3	3	3	3
2	2	2	2	2	2	2	2	2	2	2	2	2	2	2	2	2	2	2	2	2	2	2	2	2
1	1	1	1	1	1	1	1	1	1	1	1	1	1	1	1	1	1	1	1	1	1	1	1	1

Cash Cow   **Confused**   **Focused**

- Analyzing the results
  - If you are truly customer focused, you will score strong 4s and 5s on the right-hand side, while scoring 1s and 2s on the left-hand side.
  - If you treat the customer as a cash cow, you will score strong 4s and 5s on the left-hand side, while scoring 1s and 2s on the right-hand side.
  - Answers all over the map represent a confused position, which means confused customers and confused employees.
  - The reason why most organizations' results are all over the map and not consistent is because they are promising one thing (relationships with customers) and delivering something else (efficiency) instead.

We call this result *the heart attack*. If you are in the heart attack zone, it means you are causing a heart attack to your most important stakeholders, customers and employees:

- To customers, you send a message of commitment and intention, which raises their expectations. When they are faced with meager results, their disappointment and resentment is much greater than it might have been otherwise. You are better off without the great declarations, if you do not have an operation and the people to support and fulfill them.

- To employees you send a confusing and conflicting message. They hear from you that focusing on customers is critical to the company's success. However, just as they are ready to move to execution, an efficiency or self-serving instruction emerges to confuse them. After a while, they get used to the roller coaster, so they simply ignore the instructions and stick to the efficiency model, neglecting the customer in the process.

When you operate in the heart attack zone, you are not customer-centric, but you *think* you are. You have fallen into the trap of believing your own hype and jumping head first into the illusion that your declarations are followed religiously by your people. It's time to wake up and get out of the heart attack zone. That's exactly what this book is all about.

The good news is that you scored like the vast majority of the people who took this test. The bad news is that you are confusing your customers and employees, who will then treat your products or services as commodities. You have a significant opportunity to refocus on the customer and differentiate yourself from other companies. The threat is that someone else will do it before you get around to it.

In 2000, Kellogg Corporation,[4] the world leader in breakfast cereal, was losing market share and facing shrinking profit margins amid tough competition from General Mills. In a move geared toward expansion, the company decided to purchase Keebler for $4.6 billion. The logic behind the move was to reduce dependency on cereals from 75% to 40% of their overall business. In fact, what the company did was accept the commoditization forces of its market, instead of fighting for market share and finding new ways to add value for customers. As with many similar moves, this one produced results far short of expectations: Keebler sales did not provide the expected level of business.

As the situation got worse, and Kellogg's was back to its original commoditization challenge, the company discovered that it had also lost its long-guarded number-one position in market share and global leadership to General Mills, which then had 32.5% of the total market sales versus 31.2% for Kellogg. In response, Kellogg's executives came up with a brilliant idea: instead of reading the handwriting on the wall, they decided to stick to their corporate objectives. To ensure that they would not lose more market share (a factor that did not matter in the least to any of their customers), Kellogg's responded by adding more volume—more cereal—to each box, while keeping the same price and therefore keeping the *mathematical* number-one position in volume sales. As could be expected, this move resulted in further erosion of profits.

At this point, after several quarters of losses, the company decided to face the customer, instead of its self-serving objectives, and try to come up with a reason for customers to offer Kellogg's attention and money for its products. They decided to innovate and add more value. They introduced cereals with new flavors and additions, such as Special K Red Berries, and thus were able to charge nearly double the price of regular cereals. Overall, the company's margins increased, and it experienced a 52% gain in net income for 2002.

The lesson is this: if you weed out the self-serving objectives that mean nothing to customers and listen to what customers are telling you, commoditization can be challenged and new revenues achieved. However, to do so, you must face a critical decision about your objectives: will you be customer pleasers or efficiency crunchers? Unfortunately for most companies, the path to the right choice goes through many of the wrong choices.

The first choice is clear. What is the company's core competency and main business—efficiency or customer pleasing? Both may produce revenues, but efficiency will be gained at a greater cost than customer pleasing. This first choice is critical, as it dictates the path for later choices. By tuning in to the customer option, you chart a certain path for running your business; choosing efficiency will lead you onto a different path altogether. The two cannot coexist. Efficiency will help you reduce business costs; customer focus will help you increase revenues and lower the price of products. Many will argue that the two are not mutually exclusive. Although effectiveness and cost reduction can be achieved through effective customer strategies, the basic choice needs to be made, nevertheless. The tendency of companies to default to efficiency models and abuse customers in the process is chronic and embedded. The critical choice of putting the customer first must be made.

This choice may seem easy on the surface, but as you follow the rest of the choices detailed in the next chapters, you will recognize that it goes beyond lip service and requires a long-term operational commitment.

Endnotes

1. Jonathan Alter, "Press 1 to Cut Short Your Life" (New York: *Newsweek,* May 20, 2002), p. 45.

2. Strativity, CEM 2003 Annual Global Study by Strativity Group.

3. Joseph Berger, "Of Milk and Cookies, or How Orthodox Jews Saved an Italian Recipe" (New York: *New York Times* Sunday Edition, January 12, 2003), p. 27.

4. Joann Muller, "Honey, I Shrank the Box" (New York: *Forbes,* November 10, 2003), p. 82.

3

CRITICAL CHOICE 2:
WHAT IS THE ROLE OF THE CUSTOMER
IN OUR EXISTENCE?

When we examined the challenges associated with becoming customer focused (by exploring the pitfalls discovered through our research), we reached the most startling realization. The customer and the company live in distinctly different ecosystems that are inherently conflicting, like two groups of aliens living on separate planets and speaking different languages. But language is not the least critical aspect of the issue at hand. At the core of the difference between customers and companies is a completely different set of needs, concerns, wishes, and desires.

INHERENT CONFLICT

Some experts have argued that the difference is a matter of mindset, that customers and companies think differently. I beg to disagree. Our research and experience demonstrate a fundamental difference that affects not only the way customers and companies think but also the way they operate and make decisions. Companies and customers do not perceive facts and take action in accordance with the same set of considerations. Thus they are in chronic misalignment; everything they try to do together will be overshadowed by this conflict, and the likelihood of success becomes slim or perhaps even zero. The problem of becoming customer focused cannot be solved by tweaking a certain procedure or function; the conflict is inherent and requires existential examination.

When we examine the customer ecosystem, we see that it includes such factors as seeking pleasure, profit, recognition, and prestige, as well as other experience-based expectations. These factors may well be the results of product and service consumption. But customers view their benefits through the prism of the ultimate impact on their lives. They are not much concerned with how products are created, as long as the ultimate benefit will be delivered to their ultimate satisfaction. The customer ecosystem is heavily influenced by two major gravitational forces that shape the ecosystem regularly: seeking greater personalization and experiences and lower product and service prices. Products and services that qualify for greater experiences and personalization will be less affected by the need for price reduction. Products that do not qualify will be heavily influenced by the price-reduction gravitational force. The two forces are pulling in opposite directions. Those products and services that correspond to the need for experience manage to minimize the opposite force of price reductions. Those that do not correspond are subject to the price-reduction gravitational force.

The company ecosystem is focused on the product, service, or operation and thus involves a different set of factors. A production-centered company is seriously and regularly concerned with cost, research and development, channel and distribution issues, manufacturing expenses, and operational procedures, to name a few. These factors guide the daily decisions of a company's executives and determine the fate of its products and services. Management measures its success and views its core competency and financial health from the perspective of these factors. The two gravitational forces affecting the company's ecosystem are increasing margins and reducing costs of the products. These two opposing forces influence the executives' decisions and actions. In an attempt to increase margins, executives will try to sell their products at higher prices. They will also continue the cost reduction efforts to ensure that their products are competitively priced in the marketplace. In their view, the result means retaining a greater portion of profit.

As indicated in Exhibit 3.1, when placing both ecosystems with their respective gravitational forces next to one another we realize the inherent conflict. Both customers and companies live on inherently different planets. They live by different concerns and wishes. They are motivated by different factors and issues and overall their requirements are in an inherent conflict with each other. The gravitational forces requiring further cost reduction are in direct conflict with the customer wishes for further personalization of experience. Cost reduction is the company's way of accelerating the commoditization of their products and services—which results in noncompliance with the customer's demand for more experience and personalization. Naturally, the customer will be reluctant to pay a premium for the products or services and will default to the price-reduction gravitational force. Companies that attempt to raise prices to increase margins face a conflict with

Exhibit 3.1   The Inherent Conflict

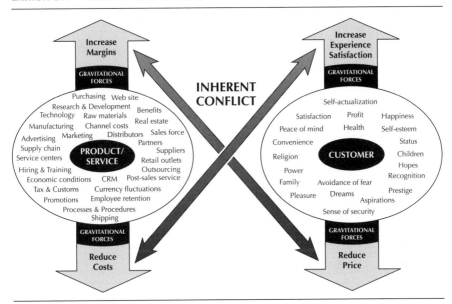

the customer's need to reduce prices. Without any special value in products and services that were commoditized by companies' cost reduction efforts, customers are left with no choice. They seek the lowest price for the already lower value provided by the company. This customer gravitational force blocks the company's need for higher prices and margins. Customers become highly sensitive to the total value proposition provided by companies; if they sense commodity, they reply with price strategy, seeking the lowest price available as the primary purchasing factor. This gravitational force, of course, is in direct conflict with the company's interest in greater margins. Companies reduce costs to increase margins, and customers seek further reduced prices for the heavily commoditized and impersonal products or services provided to them. Companies continue to operate by their own ecosystem rules, ignoring the customer's needs. This Catch 22 stems from the inherent conflict between the two entities. They simply live on different planets with different sets of interests and expectations.

The ongoing Fatal Mistakes described in Chapter 1 occur because companies and customers live on different planets. Companies are confident that they understand their customers, but in fact they follow their own rules rather than the customer's.

Understanding and accepting this inherent conflict means that companies can start to rethink their customer strategies and relationships and redesign their operations accordingly. They need to relocate to the customer's ecosystem. Companies that refuse to accept the principle of inherent conflict will continue to live in chaos, trying to compensate by short-term customer initiatives and programs. Such programs will be short lived at best and will not build long-term customer commitment. Cosmetic exercises, special sales or deals, and lack of serious commitment will only increase the conflict; customers will be further convinced that the company does not care about their concerns. It is the equivalent of building a skyscraper on shaky ground and claiming that the marble cover will compensate for the weak foundation. It is plainly and simply irrational.

THE EFFICIENT RELATIONSHIP PARADOX

When we examine companies operating in the inherent conflict zone, we often recognize the efficient relationship paradox syndrome. Before the establishment of a relationship with the customer, companies spend significant resources to court and pursue the customer through sales and marketing. Upon achieving an initial commitment in the form of a purchase, the company drops its investment level and shifts to an efficiency-based service in the name of maximizing revenues and minimizing costs. In essence, the company assumes that the investment stage is very short and that they are now able to maximize profits from the newly acquired customers, while minimizing the costs associated with maintaining these customers.

At the height of the customers' emotional and financial commitment to the company, they usually experience the lowest level of service and fulfillment of the promised relationship. When customers realize that the relationship was intended to be short term and that the company never intended to reciprocate, they begin to migrate. This migration comes in steps, which signal plans to defect. As the company eventually understands the signals, it vainly rushes in with defection-prevention programs. Now it is again facing high investment with minimal commitment from the customer. At this stage, customers are frustrated, disappointed, and less likely to buy into any promotion or offer. Even if they do, it will come at a high cost to the company, because the firm will have to forgo its margins to buy the customer back with heavy discounting.

As Exhibit 3.2 illustrates, the efficient relationship is not a reality but rather a paradox. Companies want to believe in its feasibility, but in fact only frustrate their customers in the process and lose money while at it. This is the essence of the efficient relationship paradox syndrome. Companies believe they can have a relationship that is efficient and still commands

Exhibit 3.2   The Efficient Relationship Paradox

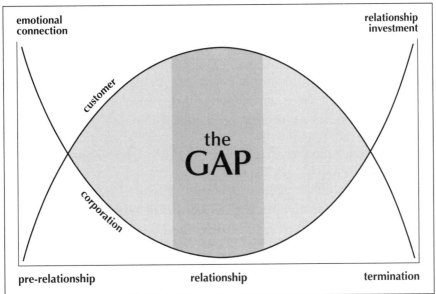

customer commitment and preference. Companies treat post-sales service as a cost against the initial sale and a threat to their precious margins, as opposed to regarding it as the most affordable sales enabler for the next purchase. This is not surprising, considering that most companies do not have a detailed plan for what to sell the customer beyond the first sale. They treat the customer as a destination that, once reached, is in safe territory and taken for granted. Customers hate to be taken for granted. When they sense it, they defect.

When we present this paradox model in our seminars, we often equate it to personal life. In the beginning both sides are investing resources, money, and creativity to lure the other side; when a commitment is achieved, there is an immediate decrease in investment. One party feels as if the pressure is off, and it's time to return to some boring existence. Then, just as the other party, who feels neglected and disappointed, is about to leave the relationship, the neglecting party tries desperate measures like buying a grand gift. This quick fix doesn't usually work—it doesn't address the underlying problem of lack of willingness to invest for the long term. This analogy usually manages to get the audience to understand and relate to the paradox.

Over time, companies become comfortable with this model. They employ actuaries to predict how many customers they can churn so they can invest more in acquiring new ones to replace them. Industry studies estimated the churn rate (rate of customers leaving the company) at an average of 20% a year (representing a 100% churn over five years). Somehow, for reasons unknown, companies are comfortable with this huge waste of investment in customer acquisition as they continue the vicious cycle. What companies fail to recognize is that over time, as the efficient relationship paradox continues, they significantly increase the cost of acquiring new customers—they have created a mass of upset customers who will badmouth them at any opportunity. These disappointed customers will create an unfavorable reputation, which will be more costly to overcome and reverse. As indicated in Exhibit 3.3, the cost of new customers grows as the company continues with its "acquire and churn" model.

The problem is that most companies do not know the cost of acquiring new customers. It is usually an allocation from a greater pool, and thus there is no way to determine the full extent of the damage caused by the efficient relationship paradox over time. This same lack of accuracy and financial data makes companies continue with the efficient relationship paradox, courting customers without knowing whether they are prone to create profits or losses. Marketing continues to claim that the cost of new customers is increasing because of market conditions and the competitive environment of the advertising market. This is the typical response of a silo-based organization when each area is involved only in its own set of objectives.

Exhibit 3.3   Lifetime View of the Efficient Relationship Paradox

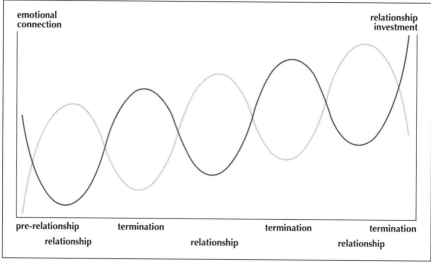

When Tom Farmer and Shane Atchison of Seattle, Washington, made a reservation at the Doubletree Club Hotel in Houston, they requested a guarantee for late arrival. Upon arrival at 2:00 in the morning, they were surprised to be told that the hotel was sold out. Even though they had a credit card guarantee and one of them was an HHonors Gold member, they were simply refused rooms. Mike, the reception person, refused to help and was rather rude. They eventually stayed at a motel on the other side of town. The night, however, was not spent sleeping. They dedicated their precious time to creating a 17-slide PowerPoint presentation detailing their view of Mike's future job prospects and the overall loss in business that the hotel would suffer as a result of their bad experience. They then sent it to 400 friends and family members and encouraged them to share the gospel. This was on November 21, 2001. On November 23, the Hilton Corporation received over 300 media inquiries, including some from CNN and other national media outlets. By the end of the first month, it was estimated that more than 1 million people had read the presentation.

Mike no longer works there, and the hotel is no longer part of the Doubletree group. But this is not the lesson. The lesson is that the power to hurt customers is much greater than you expect, and a single bad experience can have a major effect on business. No amount of advertising can erase this kind of ongoing bad-mouthing shared via the Web. The cost of new customers becomes significant as a result of the efficient relationships companies try to run while churning an average of 20% of their customers every year.

CORPORATIONS AT A JUNCTURE

Living in conflicting ecosystems and uselessly repeating the efficient relationship paradox is not a solution. This is the fastest lane to product and service commoditization and to losing market share. As much as companies complain about intense competition and shorter product life cycles, they often bring this problem on themselves by not accelerating their own product's commoditization. They decide to start shedding costly aspects and ingredients, which often create the uniqueness of their products. As opposed to innovating the products and taking them to the next level, they choose the beaten path of cost reduction and then are surprised by the customer's reluctance to pay a premium for their bland, vanilla products. In the name of efficiency, companies are taking value away from customers. The customer's response to this move is only natural and expected. Companies that are serious about their customers must face the question head on. Are we focused on our efficiency or on the customer? Is the customer the end goal or a piece of the puzzle that will make us a fortune? Are we constantly adding value or taking value from customers? In the defining moment, which comes first, our efficiency or our customers?

Before you rush to respond with a cliché, consider the following question: Who owns the customer at your company? Some executives claim it is sales or marketing, but then those operations claim they do not have full authority to execute. Others will claim it is everyone's job. I usually smile when I hear this answer. Then I further probe: "If three of your top ten customers defect to the competition, who will get fired?" At this point I get the puzzled stare, the one that says "You got me."

It is easy to claim that the customer comes first; it is much harder to execute. It requires a disciplined effort that changes many of the operational aspects to fit the customer expectations and then exceed them. Most companies believe they do what needs to be done, and yet they fail to obtain customer loyalty. Consider a large global business-to-business company with whom one of their top five accounts, worth over $100 million a year to them, shared a list of requests for improvement. The company's executives diligently wrote out the suggestions. A year later, they sent the salesperson to ask the customer to increase their purchasing volume for the following year. Knowing very well that the customer's buyer does not speak to the operations people who provided the suggestions, they were hoping the suggestions would be forgotten. It was their unlucky day. The buyer happened to check with operations. The executive who shared this story with us said it is common practice to leverage customer silo environments.

So here it is, the difficult choice. Which comes first, the customer or the company's efficiency? At the moment of truth, what would the lowest level employee of your organization do, select efficiency or customer needs? What would be the safe choice for that employee? Selecting the customer does not mean choosing unprofitable customers or just any customer. You should choose profitable customers to justify the required efforts—but the choice must be made.

Does selecting the customer come at the expense of efficiency? Companies can actually save money by listening to customer requests rather than wasting money on unfounded projects. But the priority must be set. Every employee must know what to choose when the defining moment comes. Do we follow efficiency rules and procedures or do we break the rules because the customer is the top priority? For many companies who declare customer superiority, the rest of the organization is not ready for it, and hence the heart attack results from the aptitude test in Chapter 2. Confused employees ultimately follow the money trail and do what the procedures and compensation plan dictate.

WHAT CUSTOMERS?
THE SECOND TOUGH CHOICE

As in personal life, the quality of a relationships is directly linked to the amount of intimacy and commitment. You can establish casual, short-term relationships with many, based on smalltalk and minimal commitment. A deeper, mutual, long-term relationship can be built only with a few. It is a matter of economics as well as fit. You cannot afford to have that level of commitment with too many people.

In the same way, companies can establish casual, noncommittal relationships with millions or choose to build longer, deeper relationships with a few. Because of limited resources and attention, companies cannot afford an intimate relationship with too many customers. Each company will have its individual limits, but nevertheless all have limits. Not recognizing those limits is at the core of the problem. Companies attempt to stretch their limits and, in the process, disappoint their most loyal customers. After a successful start, companies quickly become greedy. Shifting again to the efficiency model, they try to operate by numbers games and add as many customers as possible to their customer base, instead of focusing on and protecting the select few that bring the most revenues and profits.

Selecting the first option will mean a higher churn rate and a constant search for new casual partners. Selecting the latter option will allow companies to focus efforts on existing customers and build deeper relationships with them through additional investment. The same investment in resources and time that will go to find new casual partners will now be reinvested in deepening the relationships with the select few. Financially speaking, the first option is a recipe for shrinking margins and constant crisis-mode operation. The second is a path to product invention and higher revenues and margins. Not making a decision means selecting the first option by default. "The more, the merrier," say many operation-centered companies, which neglect to measure the high costs of such a choice. Costs such as churn rate and losing profitable customers to the competition, as well as the growing costs of acquiring new customers are just a few of the margin-reducing expenses inflicted by the default choice.

If this idea is common sense, why are companies not following it? Because there are very few executives who will dare to say no to a customer. There is a notion that every customer is a good customer, that everyone is a prospect. If they can spell our name and they have a budget, they are potential customers (even if they don't know that yet). Examine your sales manuals, and you will find plenty of guidelines outlining the customers on which to focus, but hardly any outlining which ones to stay away from. At the height of the Internet bubble, the situation got so bad that customers without budgets were frequently accepted. Companies rushed to establish leasing programs and bear the full cost just to close on another customer. This is, after all, the name of the game—closing, not servicing. We are all more excited about new customers than about retaining the old ones.

Can we afford to say no to a customer? No, we cannot. In reality, your product or service is not a commodity in high demand by everyone (despite your personal conviction). Not all customers are created equal. Some are profitable, and others are not. Those who are profitable are the ones who actually find value in what you sell. They are the customers who will appreciate your value proposition and be willing to pay for it. Others will not. Coercing customers into buying your products through heavy discounting will not make them appreciate your value. It will only depreciate your value in the eyes of customers who are ready and willing to pay your price. As a result of lack of selection of customers, you end up with a service that does not satisfy anyone. Those who appreciate your products and who paid a premium for them are getting unacceptable service, and those who never fully appreciated your products are receiving service they do not deserve.

If you had focused directly on the customers with whom you match the best, you would have freed up resources from caring for unsuitable customers and would have been able to deepen the relationship with the right customers. This would have partially addressed the efficient relationship paradox. By not being willing to make the tough choice, you are setting every relationship up for failure and establishing a situation of constant emergencies and crisis, when you need to "save the day" with the important customers.

Ultimately, the price of not choosing the right customers will be paid in deeper discounts and lower margins, as well as higher cost of services and greater customer defections. It also affects the ability to build products and services that are fully fitted to customer needs, as opposed to vanilla offerings that are supposed to reach the greater market and as such form the lowest common denominator. This choice affects everything the company experiences and is therefore crucial to establishing any customer strategy.

CONGRATULATIONS, YOU ARE AT PAR: THE NEW FOUR Ps

The traditional four Ps of marketing, Product, Placement, Price, and Promotion, were subjected to massive depreciation in the last few years. None of them now provide a sustainable differentiation that justifies loyalty and customer commitment. Although companies are still laboring to provide good products and competitive prices available at many locations and promoted through multiple vehicles and media, none of these efforts registers as special in customers' minds. Companies often allocate the vast majority of their resources to these traditional Ps, only to find themselves at par with customer expectations. At par means undifferentiated and therefore not preferred.

Any new product launched in the marketplace is subject to significant and ever growing competitive forces. The uniqueness of the product will wear off much sooner than it would have 20 years ago. The auto industry has been sharing core competency for years and has developed and manufactured cars together to reduce costs. To respond to retailer demand, many national brands began to manufacture private labels, which ended up by diluting the differentiation of their own products. Add to these trends the ubiquitous availability of products through the Web, and a product's differentiation becomes a less defendable position and more of a rite of passage.

The recent surge in availability of cheaper medicines through virtual pharmacies in Canada, Mexico, and elsewhere is another wake-up call for the diminishing effects of placement as a differentiator. Customers will find what they want on their own terms, when and where they want to. The Web allows every customer, regardless of location, to obtain their desired products at the best available prices, so there goes another bastion of marketing leadership.

It's time to move beyond the at-par line. It's time to face the emerging new Ps, around which each company must build leadership and core competency:

- Premium price
- Preference of company or product
- Portion of overall customer budget
- Permanence of overall relationship longevity

Unlike the old four Ps, which represented the company's choices and decisions and were driven by the company's actions, these four Ps are driven by customer actions and finally incorporate customers into the center of a company's principles. Therefore, they are a true measure of the company's overall strength, as they represent the active vote of confidence of their most important asset, the people who pay the bill—the revenue makers. (I have always found it strange and disturbing that most companies regard their salespeople and not their customers as the revenue makers.)

Premium price is about your ability to charge and obtain a higher price. It signifies that the product is perceived by the customer as superior, differentiated, and, most of all, worth their business. Customers buy many products they need for their everyday life, but only a few of those products command premium prices. From the customers' perspective, the fact that a product commands a premium price does not necessarily make it special; thus such products are often purchased at discount. By managing to obtain a premium price the customer bypasses the discount alternative and reaffirms his conviction in the value delivered by the premium priced product. Companies that do not command a premium price are on a downward spiral toward cost cutting, value depreciation, and reduced margins.

Only the premium-priced products are the ones that the customer is actively voting for through willingness to pay the premium. This active vote of confidence is what makes this measure critical to the new customer-centric companies.

Preference for products and services goes beyond selection of a product. Many products are selected daily by millions of customers, temporarily, until a better option appears in the marketplace. Living on borrowed time is not a way to manage a business.

True product preference involves providing referrals to friends and peers, as well as a willingness to support the product publicly. Public support may include endorsement, press interviews, and sharing your opinions via web channels. The customer lends personal credibility to the product and assists the company in selling it. This is a greater level of action, going beyond a personal financial sacrifice (premium price). How do you know whether your product commands preference? Simply examine and ensure your cost of sales and see how often and how many referrals you get free of charge from satisfied customers. Stating satisfaction is easy; providing referrals is harder and requires action. If your product commands premium overtime you will see cost of sales dropping and margins increasing.

Portion of budget is another critical customer action area. It's all about providing your company with a larger portion of the customer's total budget. As long as there are competitors, customers may share their budget among several vendors. This is usually a sign that they lack a preference and don't think that one company deserves their loyalty. When a customer provides one vendor with a greater share over competing vendors, it is a clear sign of commitment. Every company must first benchmark their current share of budget, seek to build value, and measure success through their overall share of customer budget.

Permanence, as in personal relationships, is the ultimate measure. The longer a customer stays with a vendor, the deeper the relationship becomes and the more invested he or she is in the relationship. Although many companies state that their goal is longer, more profitable relationships, they often fail to obtain them. The reason is this: companies do not place enough emphasis on the permanency aspect and often let it die. Beyond the initial selling campaign, companies do not structure and build a program to retain the relationship for the long term. They expect permanence to happen by itself and hope that the initial excitement will last on its own. Customers sense that they are being taken for granted, and thus they seek another provider, who has a willingness to serve and provide an exciting experience.

Another reason for short relationships is lack of excitement in the company's overall value proposition. In the name of maximizing revenues and profits and minimizing costs, companies extend the life of their products and do not innovate and revive them—thus they become boring. Bored customers do not stay long. Boring products and services are another signal that a relationship has been taken for granted.

Permanence needs to be planned. As in personal life, you will not keep your loved ones by doing the same old thing over and over again. You definitely will not establish a long-term relationship on the basis of efficiency and lack of renewal. The customer excitement threshold is lower than ever, and customers will switch faster than ever, unless you give them a fresh and exciting reason to stay. Unlike a one-time trick, permanence reflects a deeper relationship, with long-term commitment. The customer will call your bluff faster than you think. Inertia toward customers is not a strategy—it is living on borrowed time.

Manchester United has one of the most impressive customer-based programs we have found.[1] Manchester United is one of the most popular sports franchises in the world. The British-based team boasts 53 million fans around the world. But its fans have a unique way to demonstrate their loyalty and commitment to the team, which goes far beyond attending games and purchasing sports shirts and memorabilia. Fans have the choice of participating in financial products. Credit cards, mortgages, and savings accounts are some of the branded products offered to fans through association with a local bank. The fans who place their money in the savings account are taking a small risk. Their interest rate may be determined on the basis of the team's performance. If Manchester United qualifies to the premiership games, a certain interest rate will be applied to their savings accounts. If the team progresses to the semifinals, a different rate will be applied. If the team wins the premiership or the European championship, the fans will share in the winning, which will be reflected in their savings account interest. Although somewhat different from programs in other industries, the principle remains the same: customer actions determine the true level of loyalty to the company. Customers who are satisfied will put their money where their mouth is. The fans of Manchester United do it.

Choosing the customer means choosing to be in a relationship not because of necessity, but because it is what we want to do. It is a mission and a source of satisfaction. Choosing the right customers and saying no to the rest will be a critical litmus test of your commitment to the first choice. Selecting all customers who are willing to pay implies casual, short-term relationships. Customers will quickly recognize your real intentions and will reciprocate. No company can survive in the long term on such casual, temporary relationships. Without selection, customers will default, and companies will begin the downward spiral of accelerated commoditization. That path must be avoided at all costs. Therefore, selecting those customers who fit our plans is a critical step toward building a customer-centric organization.

Endnote

1. *www.manutd.com.*

4

CRITICAL CHOICE 3:
WHAT DEFINES OUR TOTAL EXPERIENCE?

When the Managing Customer Relationships programs first began to evolve, the basic assumptions were flawed: the programs were not focused on the customer. Let's start with a simple question: were the customers asked whether they wanted to be in a relationship, or were they merely picked because of their previous purchasing patterns and forced to undergo an intensive assault to sell them more? The answer in most cases is that customers were never asked if they were willing participants in the relationship, but were instead taken for granted.

In addition, the long list of technologies developed in the name of customer relationships never provided any way for customers to talk back to their relationship partners. Companies would communicate on their own terms, in their desired tone and preferred time frame. The sole purpose of the communication was to sell more, not to build a better *mutual* relationship. What kind of a relationship is it, when one side is dominant, to the level of abuse, and the other side is hardly allowed to speak up?

Probably the most arrogant assumptions of all were that the customer already loved the value proposition, that the company's products and services were already superior, and that selling more was the main aim. Such arrogant underlying assumptions meant that the company did not try to improve the value proposition and experiences—thus winning customers—but instead tried to tweak their selling tactics to move more products.

Let's take a moment to examine some of the core customer-centric terms. "Loyalty," "experience," and "relationships" are emotionally loaded terms. They represent a certain level of commitment that transcends logic and numbers. When a customer is asked for loyalty, he or she is asked to bypass logical considerations such as price and still prefer a certain product or vendor. These core terms do not correspond well to a corporate, numbers-oriented environment. They represent absolute commitments. An understanding of that fact is crucial to understanding our expectations from customers and what we are required to provide in return. Customers do not split their loyalty into pie charts and graphs, the usual corporate measurements of loyalty. For a customer it is either Pepsi or Snapple. When we speak in terms of relationships and experiences, we signal that we are seeking an absolute commitment, an emotionally loaded one that will transcend prices in return for greater value delivered. We want customers to appreciate the value we provide and commit to our products even if they are more expensive. This is a lot to ask. It requires reciprocation. It requires that we deliver significant value in return.

If we think of ourselves as customers, we can ask: what is loyalty all about? It is about a strong relationship that creates a nonfinancial preference. We place emotions above the logical price comparison. Loyalty is a result of a strong relationship that guides our preferences and decisions.

What drives a strong relationship? A strong relationship is made of the basic building blocks of *experiences*. Consistently positive and exciting experiences will lead to stronger relationships. Inconsistent and disappointing experiences will lead to weak relationships. These experiences happen everywhere and across multiple touch points in the organization. Each experience impacts on the "relationship account" with the customer. A deposit will mean a positive and exciting experience. A withdrawal is the result of a negative experience or a request for additional purchases. The concept of the relationship account can help companies to understand their customer relationships better. When every interaction is either a withdrawal or a deposit, it is easier to see the importance of each interaction and experience. Deposits should be made generously, and withdrawals should be made carefully. Although many companies measure their experiences in terms of features, the maximum-impact experiences are the ones created by people, not machines. The experiences that make the greatest impact on the relationship account are the most intense and pleasing. Yes, an IVR automated response system in a call center is a form of an experience — it touches the customer. But it is less likely to contribute to the relationship account and quite likely to make a withdrawal from it.

The best experience creators (and hence depositors to the relationship account) are people, the people who add value and personalization to the products and services, thus enhancing the company's perceived value in the eyes of the customer. They enrich the relationship account and enable the company to make more withdrawals.

Exhibit 4.1   Customer Strategy Process

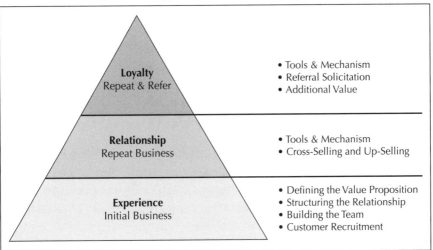

As indicated in Exhibit 4.1, there are three stages to the customer strategy process. At the bottom of the pyramid is the experience, the core value proposition across all touch points. It is this experience that determines the customer's preference and the price he or she is willing to pay. Next is the relationship stage, when further relationships are forged between customers and companies. After the initial purchase, both sides decide whether this relationship will lead to a longer commitment of repeatable business. At the loyalty stage, both sides are committed and are nurturing the already strong relationship to ensure ongoing commitment. When we view the nature of customer strategies through this prism of the strategy process, many company actions become clearer. Companies tend to focus on the relationship and loyalty stages, but our experience has shown that the problem lies at a deeper, more existential and fundamental level: the level of the experience and value proposition.

Because they are unplanned and inconsistent, company experiences fail to deliver on the promise; meaningful deposits are not made into the relationship account. In this chapter, we will focus on experiences, since they are the basic building blocks of the whole relationship. Proper design and management of those experiences will lead to a stronger, more profitable relationship. Bringing the corporate focus back to basics is critical for building successful customer strategies. Because of the false assumptions of the Customer Relationship Management evolution, we will focus our efforts on customer experience management. After all, it is up to the companies to create and deliver experiences; it is the customer who chooses the relationship. After examining the experiences delivered, the customer can choose to be in a relationship and can also choose the degree of participation. Companies can influence this choice by focusing on their experiences, differentiating them, and ensuring that they will exceed expectations.

CUSTOMER STRATEGIES AND THE ART OF CUSTOMER EXPERIENCE MANAGEMENT

Customer experience management (CEM) is a business strategy that focuses on the holistic value proposition and experience delivered to the customer. It is a customer strategy that emphasizes relationships above expectations and features as a way to differentiate and command premium price and preference. When complimented once about Nordstrom's legendary customer commitment, the department store CEO responded angrily, stating that loving the customer is not about being nice to her. It is about being greedy. He claimed that the strategy of honoring and delivering service beyond expectations is Nordstrom's way of differentiating and creating customer commitment and equity. It is essential to understand that customer strategies are not just about being nicer to people; it is a strategy of maximizing revenues and profits through customer delight.

Creating, delivering, and managing experiences beyond expectations are important. They cut across all touch points in the organization and lie at the core of every organization's relationship with customers. They are the source of establishing a relationship based on one or more of the key Ps: Preference, Premium Price, Portion of Budget, and Permanence.

One of the common mistakes regarding CEM is that it is a matter of quality customer service. Customer service is only one component of CEM—and often not the most powerful or high-impact component. By assuming that CEM resides in the customer service department, the rest of the company excuses itself from responsibility for the customer experience. We have seen repeated evidence that companies are improving service quality, yet losing customers and loyalty through other touch points with customers, such as billing and invoicing. Although important, customer service is not the point at which the problem starts, nor should the problem necessarily be solved here, either. The nature of the customer service is merely an indicator of problems and symptoms, not the root cause. Organizations that are keen on obtaining customer loyalty must drive their customer strategy across the whole organization and not just through convenient scapegoats such as customer service.

Another common mistake is to treat CEM as a "nice to have," costly frosting on top of the company's efficient operation, the kind of magic bullet you use only when all other options have been exhausted. CEM is not about peppering some extra taste into the existing mix of products. It is not a branding exercise to beautify a rather nasty operation. It is at the core of the value proposition. It *is* the value proposition. It's what you sell and what customers buy. It's what determines the price you can charge and the length of a relationship you will have. In times when the basic functionality of products and services is commoditized faster than ever, the experience is the core of the value proposition, the complete value delivered to customers and not just a single deliverable in the form of a product or service. Early product design, the quality of manufacturing, the people at the retail stores, the invoices, the quality of the legal contracts, the shipping people, and the customer service professionals—all are integral parts of the customer experience. All require design, monitoring, management, and regular evolution. CEM is about defining your core competence across your whole organization and evolving it ahead of the competition. It is about loving your customers so much with everything you have to offer that they have no reason to go elsewhere or consider other providers.

For many executives, customer relationships and customer experiences are just a set of customer surveys. Companies have conducted many listening sessions. Shrinking customer commitments to these sessions demonstrate that they are, at best, an insult to customer intelligence. Although important, listening to customers through surveys or other methods is only a sliver of what a customer strategy is all about. And if companies plan to stay at the listening level and claim that they are customer focused, they are better off without the listening. At least they will not fool themselves.

As discussed before, customers are going to the extreme. Recognizing the efficiency model in corporations and the vanilla (i.e., boring) products and services provided as a result of the efficiency focus, they reciprocate. They develop an efficiency model of their own: a discount strategy. It is not that they do not appreciate value, they simply cannot see any. In the absence of differentiation and reasons to pay a premium, they default to price as the primary decision factor.

Companies simply forgot to create and add value. They took their success for granted. They wanted to maximize their original product and service investments and then let them sit there without updating until they became irrelevant, boring, and—as we like to say in professional jargon—mature and tired. Tired products represent tired companies: companies that prefer to succumb to market trends instead of redefining them; companies that focus on incremental, existential improvements rather than order-of-magnitude change; companies that believe they still have time to milk their existing products. They are hanging on by a thread, literally waiting for a brand new competitor to hit them with a brand new, exciting value proposition that will tip the scales and push their product into the irrelevance abyss.

Exhibit 4.2 provides a pictorial view of the CEM development and management process, which is not a superficial cross-selling effort, but rather an in-depth assessment and creation of the core experience and relationships at the value proposition level. The process also takes the organizational aspects into account, as well as readiness for a customer-centric strategy. After the development and building the right organization stages, delivery of the promised experiences and relationships is detailed, with the purpose of ensuring full, mutual, and equal relationships. As with any other successful strategy, a redefine process is a must. Because customers and experience are dynamic rather than static, companies should never count on their past success; they must continue to reinvent themselves and their experience to stay relevant and attractive to customers. Corresponding to the ever evolving nature of the customer, markets, and competition, the CEM strategic

Exhibit 4.2   Customer Experience Management Process

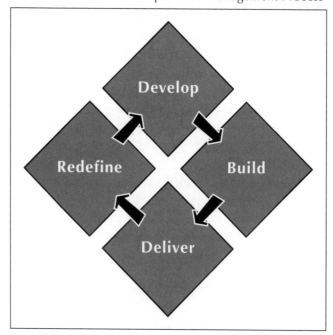

process is designed as an evolving business strategy that consists of several components:

- *Develop.* The first is development of the differentiated, beyond-expectations experiences that are most likely to command a premium, gain references, and build permanence-based relationships. During the *develop* stage, companies must address fundamental high-touch questions such as which customers to pursue and which to neglect. Appealing to mass markets usually results in dilution of experience because it needs to appeal to the lowest common denominator. Therefore, selection is key to the development of the experience. We must ensure that we establish relationships with customers who appreciate and are willing to pay for the rich experiences we design and deliver. The development stage includes customer segmentation, when we develop different flavors of the experience for different customers. Treating different customers differently is another essential principle of successful customer strategies. Treating all customers the same misses the point regarding the individuality and uniqueness of each customer and his or her needs.

- *Build.* Building the organization that can deliver the experiences is critical. The experience resides within your organization; the quality of the people, their training, and their compensation all contribute to the ability of the organization to deliver on the promise. Many customer strategies fail because of a mismatch between the designed experiences and the organization that exists to support them. The organization breathes life into the experiences, so it must be in complete sync with the steps required to focus on the customer. Confusing procedures trip up employees who are trying to do the right thing. Misaligned compensation often becomes an obstacle, and a silo mentality is another common, organization-related inhibitor to successful customer strategies.

- *Deliver.* After well-designed experiences and relationships, and aligned organization, the moment of truth comes at delivery. Often the delivery mechanism does not allow for a mutually respectful dialogue with customers. It does not treat the customer as a true partner, but rather as a secondary participant. It is crucial to build true dialogue systems that hold the company accountable to the customer, ignite feedback, and address the critical checkpoints in the customer relationships. During the delivery phase, there are several key checkpoints that each company must pass successfully to demonstrate commitment to customers. The customer will be carefully examining the company's true intentions. Only those that pass the checkpoints will win the customer's heart (and wallet).

- *Redefine.* Every well-executed experience or relationship is dynamic. Multiple sources—both internal and external—influence these relationships and require an examination of their relevance. From competitive forces and changes to customer tastes and available income—the experience must be reevaluated on a regular basis to ensure that it stays at the cutting edge and hence remains an experience that is differentiated and preferred by customers. The redefine process should take place regularly, especially during times of success. It is at the moment of glory that companies default to cost reduction and maximizing profits and fail to innovate and move to the next level; then they allow new competitors to penetrate their markets and take over the customers.

DEMYSTIFYING THE EXPERIENCE

Experiences are the sum of all the values provided to customers by the company. They run the gamut, from the initial brochure or advertising initiated by marketing to the final invoice sent by accounting. From the web site to the implementation person, every way that a company touches the customer contributes to the total experience, and hence the total value of the company's product and services. Unlike the way companies think about customers (in pie charts and graphs), customers perceive their experience and make decisions differently. When you sit down in a restaurant and the waiter asks if you want something to drink, your response is not going to be "23.4% Pepsi, 35.6% Coke, and the rest Tropicana Orange Juice." This is the view adopted by corporations when they discuss the customer and their preferences. But the customer is going to respond with either Pepsi or Coke. Customers think in black and white. Their decisions are 100% either for this vendor or for the other.

Exhibit 4.3 illustrates some basic truth regarding the nature and creation of concepts such as experience, loyalty, and relationships. Let's examine the concept of loyalty. If we understand that it is absolute in the eyes of customers, what is loyalty? Loyalty is a representation of the strength of the relationship. The stronger it is, the stronger the commitment and the loyalty. What builds a strong relationship? Strong relationships are not the result of a one-time even;, they are an ongoing process. The building blocks of a

Exhibit 4.3   Experience Evolution and Creation

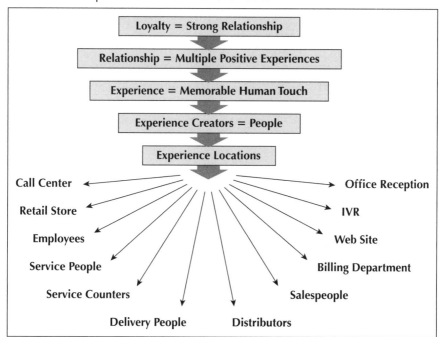

relationship are the experiences. The more we have, the stronger the relationship; the more positive and surprising the experiences, the better the relationship; the more consistent the experiences, the more likely it is that the relationship will create loyalty and commitment. Relationships, therefore, are the result of the basic building block of experiences.

I am often amazed by the way companies promote relationship tools and strategies while failing to address the basic experiences from which they are built. I am also amazed by the variety of relationship initiatives and strategies that hardly provide any room for the customer to speak up, and never ask customers if they want to be in a relationship. They simply take the customer for granted and attack them with more customized offers to maximize sales.

It is crucial to understand that although multiple cues will create an experience, the most powerful influencers on the quality and intensity of an experience are people. They are the true experience creators. One of the best illustrations of the power of the people is in your call centers. When you step into the local bank branch, you are surrounded by multiple experience cues, such as the bank's design and layout, the logo and the colors, the people who work there, the furniture, and the signage around you. Ultimately it will be the service you receive that will determine the experience quality. However, when you call the same bank's toll-free number, none of the surrounding cues will be there. The whole experience will be riding on a single factor, the voice of the customer service representative. In your mind this voice will equal the bank's reputation, its willingness to help you, and ultimately the value you receive. This is how powerful people are in experience creation.

Experiences are dynamic. They move on a scale of customer emotions like a pendulum, from the "wow" to the "never again." Exhibit 4.4 illustrates the dynamic nature of the experience and demonstrates its impact across aspects such as memorability and impact on loyalty. Great experiences will make a major financial impact on both referrals and additional business. Bad experiences will lead to a negative financial impact, both in terms of losing business and in terms of a bad or damaged reputation. Failing to understand the emotional aspect of the experience is like failing to understand customers. The number-one mistake companies make when dealing with customer experiences is focusing them on the uneventful. For the sake of closing cases and conducting transactions, companies focus their people efforts on the basic resolutions and transactions that are not memorable and thus make a negative impact on customer loyalty. If anything, they leave the door open for a competitor to come and deliver a better experience that will capture the customer's imagination and wallet. Each time a company

Exhibit 4.4   Dynamics of Experiences

Phases	Feelings	Memorability	Impact on Loyalty
Wow	"I love it"	High	Share with many
Enjoyable	"I like it"	Mid	Share with few
Functional	"Works for me"	Low	Neutral
Uneventful	"OK"	None	Decrease
Missed it	"I don't like it"	Mid	66% Decrease
Never again	"I hate it"	High	100% Loss

conducts an uneventful experience, it literally invites the competition into its home base. By not providing customers with positive emotions and excitement, the company bores them and sends them looking for better experiences elsewhere.

THE EMOTIONAL CUSTOMER

Emotions make the corporate world uncomfortable. The perception is that since emotions cannot be managed very well and are difficult to fit into pie charts or reports, they must be ignored. The efficiency-oriented operations we pride ourselves on are full of logic and predictability, so we tend to treat the customer accordingly. Financial managers have no clue as to how to factor emotions into their financial models. Thus emotions are treated as the type of irrational behavior from which we must shy away.

In reality, that thought process is fundamentally flawed. Businesses built on logic alone will be very expensive to operate. We actually want emotions in our relationships with customers. A purely logical customer will shop for the lowest price every time and will demonstrate no loyalty at all. The cost of doing business with customers will be high, because each time we will have to "acquire" them again through expensive incentives.

When we speak of relationships, loyalty, and experiences, we must remember that these are emotionally loaded terms. We borrowed them from personal relationships; individuals usually prefer a deeper commitment to a single individual over shallow relationships with many. Relationship means making an emotional selection and sticking with it. The stronger the relationship, the longer it lasts and the deeper the commitment. This is exactly what we want our customers to do with our products and services. We want them to develop a deeper, longer commitment to our brands, even if they are not the cheapest on the market.

The problem with emotions, however, is that many of them occur in a nurturing environment. They demand *mutual* commitment in order to *deliver* commitment. In the long, uncomfortable affair companies have with emotions, they have tended to exploit the *customer's* emotions but not to communicate their *own*. This is probably why very few companies will put emotions in their name, as Southwest Airlines did with the symbol LUV.

It is time to face emotions and understand that they are a strength and not a weakness. It is also time to realize that even if you cannot place it in a pie chart, it does not mean it does not exist. Understand that relationships and loyalty require reciprocity, and you, the company, need to initiate the relationship.

So unleash the power of emotions to create differentiation in your products or services. Allow your people to add their emotional touch to the overall customer experience, and by doing so, create preference and positive experiences in your customers' hearts. Build a mechanism that demonstrates to customers your sincerity and authenticity, so they will be willing to forgo the next price cut from the competition and prefer your products— despite the higher price.

Emotional customers are not problematic customers. These are customers who care; customers who share their views with the world; customers who pay you a premium and stay for the long run. They are usually profitable customers. How will you know when you get there? Just like many other important things in life, you will know it when you see it.

DEVELOPING THE EXPERIENCE

Because of the wide variety of alternatives available to their customers, companies often feel they can no longer create any differentiation. They are stuck thinking that all that can be done was done already. They feel as if their products or services have reached the heart of commoditization.

Exhibit 4.5 provides a view of the four alternatives facing any company experiencing the threat and challenges of commoditization. One is to add value prior to the purchase (early in the food chain). For example, if you are a fabric manufacturer, you may want to consider joining the fashion designers before they select the fabrics. Offer your knowledge to add value and create unique designs and fabrics that help them differentiate. If you take this road, you are likely to have a jump on the competition, either by defining the criteria for selection or by winning the contract without any competition at all. By helping fashion designers obtain unique rather than commoditized fabrics, you will tap into their ecosystem and create a unique experience of success for *them*. They repay you by buying and preferring your products.

By adding value before the purchase, your experiences evolve and become customized to customer needs, and not just another option from a long list. Your expertise and knowledge become the differentiators that add value to customers.

A second alternative is to add value after the purchase. Enrich your product with additional, post-sale services that differentiate it and deliver a more complete experience to the customer. Take care of the larger picture for your customer and minimize the assembling of value he or she needs to

Exhibit 4.5 At the Heart of Commoditization

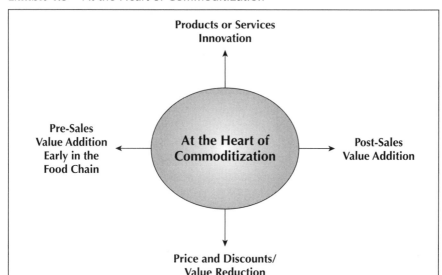

do across different service providers. This time-saving and seamless integration will customize the experience. It will command a premium price and preference from your customers.

A third alternative is to innovate. When Thomas Pink,[1] the British shirt purveyor, was looking into new product ideas, the company tapped into the customer mind set and created "The Day After Package." The package was targeted at a single male who needed a new shirt after staying overnight outside the home. It included a shirt as well as some toiletries and shaving tools, so the customer could show up at the office without the traditional stares and gossip ("Isn't he wearing the same shirt as yesterday?"). Innovating around customer needs and life events is a choice that can command premium price and preference. The surprised customers will be pleased to see that someone else did the thinking for them.

There is a fourth—and lazy—alternative: discounting. Being lazy or cautious, most companies quickly enter into this familiar terrain. It's one thing they can do easily and get quick results. But it is costly in the long term.

The choice in any event, is yours: what position do you want to take? There are different ways to get out of the heart of commoditization. Needless to say, this chapter will focus on the first three options. Somehow, we are confident that if you default to the fourth option you will know what to do without our advice.

CUSTOMER EXPERIENCE ANALYSIS

The purpose of this analysis is to map the complete value proposition of your experience, as well as to identify the differentiating (and hence premium) features of your overall customer experience. Knowing them will allow you to focus on the areas that your customer appreciates most and expand them to retain the status of a preferred product or service.

This is another exercise in viewing your product from the customer's perspective in order to create a value proposition and experiences that will keep customers coming back and paying more.

INSTRUCTIONS: List all of your product's or service's features in the space below. Include in the list every item you can think of, including some that may be perceived as mundane features, such as issuing invoices or providing post-sales support.

_____

_____

_____

_____

_____

_____

_____

_____

INSTRUCTIONS: Next, map all the features on the chart in Exhibit 4.6 according to the following criteria:

Existence Attributes. Basic features that are shared by all your competitors. If you are Nike shoes, existence attributes will be designing and manufacturing shoes, distribution channels, and a web site, for example—these are all merely a rite of passage. If you do not have them, you are not actually in the shoe manufacturing business. These attributes will not send any customer to share your greatness with others or pay a premium price for your products.

Undifferentiated Attributes. Features that are somewhat unique but that some competitors have as well. These are often innovative features that eventually were provided by some of your competitors as well. In the case of Nike, a variety of shoes in different colors that address different needs

Exhibit 4.6   The Customer Experience Analysis

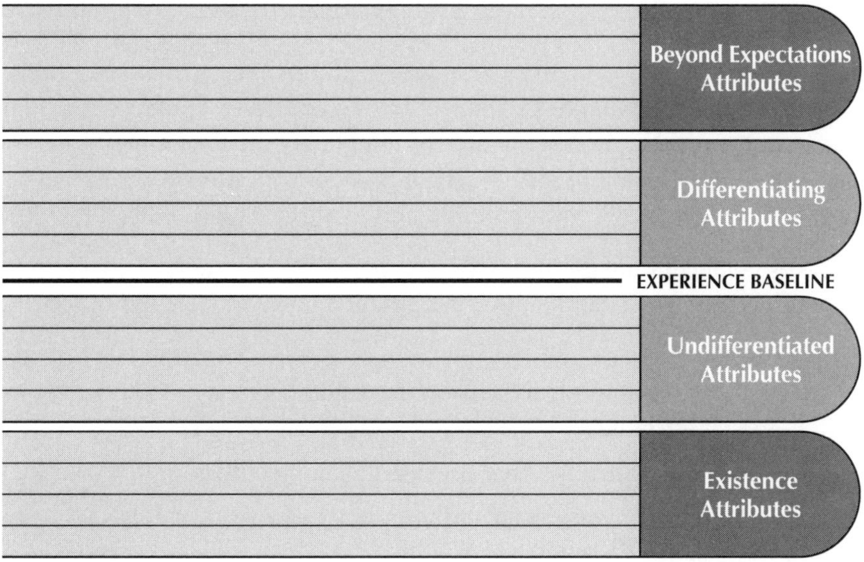

will qualify as an undifferentiated attribute. At this point, you deliver before-the-sale value to customers and manage to command some preference as a result of it. These attributes, however, still do not create strong preference, command premium price, or cause customer evangelism. These attributes represent your efforts to survive in a highly competitive landscape and capture greater market share. As a rule of thumb, if your attribute is also offered by the competition in a similar way, it is an undifferentiated attribute.

Differentiated Attributes. Innovative, unique attributes that only your product has. These are the attributes that will command premium price and will cause a customer to ignore cheaper alternatives and pay for your products. When the Nike Air technology was introduced, it commanded premium price because it was unique in the market and captured customers' imagination (and, therefore, their wallets). For a certain period, it was a differentiating attribute. When the technology was copied by competitors, the attribute dropped to the undifferentiated level. Availability of similar attributes from competitors usually results in price pressures and commoditization.

Above and Beyond Attributes. Attributes that make your customers recommend your products to other people. At this stage, your customer moves from the private domain of paying a premium price for your products to the public domain of becoming an evangelist. These attributes give you a combination of an ambassador, a promoter, and a consultant to others—all at no charge to you. The customer will rave about your products and tell others to follow his or her lead and obtain your product or service. This is the most difficult attribute to create and sustain. When Nike introduced the Air Jordan, it created a buzz through exclusivity and bold design that gave the product a "beyond expectations" attribute. Customers not only paid a premium for it but also shared it lavishly with friends and family to become the company's most credible and enthusiastic promoters.

Now that you have completed the analysis, let's review the results. If you have many features above the baseline, ask yourself the following questions:

- Do those attributes truly exist in our company today or are they aspirational attributes?
- Are all these attributes not provided by competitors?
- Do these attributes command premium price or merely allow us to sell more for the same price?
- Do we really generate more business as a result of these attributes?

As you take a more honest look at these attributes, you may choose to drop some of them below the experience baseline. In reality, most companies will find 95% of their attributes below the experience baseline. Such attributes, which represent their daily operation and existence, do not register on the customer's radar screen. They are not exciting experiences, but merely boring, bland services and products doomed to have their prices continue to decline.

As we conduct this exercise with clients, they are almost always shocked to discover the harsh reality that what they hold dear hardly makes a difference to 95% of their customers. In short, their "good" is not good enough. They are in survival mode with ever-accelerating commodities. It is a sobering exercise to many.

The few that identify some differentiating attributes are asked to identify the time frame during which they believe they will hold on to those attributes. This usually ranges between 6 to 18 months. They then realize that even their competitive advantage is on borrowed time.

The accelerated pace of innovation and copying of features have the result that most feature-based differentiators are only temporary relief, not a sustainable attribute to create lasting differentiation. Yet many companies still want to believe in feature-based differentiation. Although important, features are not sufficient, being highly dependent on a critical factor: people.

The sustainable differentiators that register *well* above the experience base-line are people driven. These are employees who care to do their best, be it in innovating the products or services or delivering outstanding customer service.

Companies that seek lasting, sustainable, differentiating attributes must reexamine their employees' experiences to determine how to build human-driven attributes into their value proposition consistently. This goes beyond the tired old story of the one employee who dared to break the rules. This is about building an entire *operation* of rule breakers. It requires a different culture and conditions for such behavior to be nourished and cultivated.

CUSTOMER EXPERIENCE MAPPING

Now we need to examine new ways to develop differentiating value propo-sitions and experiences. To do so, we need to wear the customer's glasses and take the perspective from which the customer sees our products and services. We also need to explore the language in which a customer describes and thinks about them. The purpose of this exercise is to allow you to see your products and services from the customer's viewpoint. When you do so, you will be surprised to discover your real competition and identify your real business. You will be able to broaden your value proposition and consider new ways to create a *differentiated* value proposition.

In the hotel example in Exhibit 4.7, we can see that from a features viewpoint, the hotel provided similar value for all four customer segments. All the customers in the four different segments consumed space (rooms, conference rooms) and food. However, when we examine the associated emotions and aspirations, we see a wide discrepancy. Business travelers described their consumption of hotel features using words such as loneli-ness, fear of failure, and powerlessness. Nonresidents (people who come to drink a cup of coffee in the lobby, but do not stay over to sleep in a room) described their aspirations and emotions in words such as convenience, image, and embarrassment. Thus the definition of the hotel's real business varied widely, depending on which customers it serviced.

On weekdays the hotel was in the executive effectiveness business, competing against personal assistants, video conferencing, and spas. On the weekends it was in the marital counseling business, competing with trips abroad, psychiatrists, and sex toys. Approaching the business from the fea-tures standpoint would not result in outstanding experiences. By defining the business from the customer's views, emotions, and aspirations, we can now see that there are greater choices customers perceive are available to

Exhibit 4.7   Customer Experience Mapping: Hotel Chain Example

	COMPETITORS	
Temporary office space, internal meeting space, entertainment complex		Spas, long-term stay, teleconferences, video conferences, personal assistants

	REAL BUSINESS	
Business Enablement		Executive Effectiveness & Confidence

EMOTIONS/ASPIRATIONS

	FEATURES				
• Loss of money • Embarrassment • Teamwork • Confidence • Stress • Fear of losing jobs	• Meeting Space • Food • Accessories	**CUSTOMERS** Conferences & Meetings	Business Travelers	• Beds • Food & Beverages • Internet Connection • Health Club	• Loneliness • Fear of failure • Estrangement • Loss of control • Powerlessness • Stress
• Low-level image • Embarrassment • Discomfort to do business • Lack of convenience • Change from office boredom • Work stress	• Food & Beverages • Meeting Space—Unpaid	Non Residents	Leisure Travelers	• Beds • Food & Beverages • Health Club	• Boredom • Stagnation • Need to escape • Rejuvenation • Marital stress

Image and Work Improvement		Marriage Counseling & Stress Reduction
Cafes, restaurants, temporary office, own office		Amusement parks, trip abroad, marriage counselors, movies, sports events

address the desired emotions and aspirations. To fulfill the need for relaxation or escape, customers can attend music concerts, travel abroad, buy a video game, go to amusement parks, or just read a good book. The choice to fulfill the relaxation need will not just be staying at a getaway hotel. As such the hotel competes with a larger relaxation provider and not just the next-door hotel. This greater set of competitors can deliver new ideas about how to redefine your experiences to be in sync with the customer's mind set, rather than being driven by your operational focus. Being in sync will in turn lead to premium services and products that can enhance your presence above the experience baseline.

We can also see that segmentation reveals hidden value not visible from a feature-set standpoint. If the hotel's perception is that its business is in the space and food markets, it completely misses the possibilities that come with viewing different customers differently. The hotel will miss out on opportunities to provide for the small- to mid-size businesses or the bored couples who frequent their hotel but are facing bland offerings that do not really meet their needs. These customers end up settling for less because the alternative is not much better.

Exhibit 4.8   Customer Experience Mapping

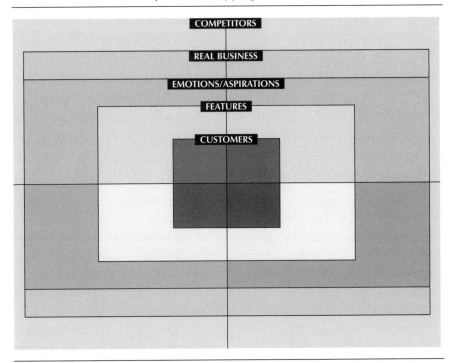

INSTRUCTIONS: Following the example given in Exhibit 4.8, fill in the blanks on the map by following the instructions below:

1. In the box titled "Customers," list a single customer segment your organization pursues.

2. In the box titled "Features," list the products or services you sell to that segment.

3. Then ask yourself, "What are the emotions and aspirations associated with my product or service?" and record your answers in the box titled "Emotions/Aspirations."

4. Based on your observations about how your product or service satisfies your customers' emotional needs or desires, ask yourself, "What is my real business from the customer's perspective?" and record your answer in the box titled "Real Business."

5. Finally, fill in the box titled "Competition" by answering the questions, "What are the customer's alternatives to my products? Who are my competitors, from the customer's perspective?"

After this exercise, you may reach several conclusions:

- When you view different customers differently, you can create better, more suitable experiences for customers, as opposed to sinking to the lowest common denominator.
- Customized services based on emotions and aspirations should allow you better connection and communication with customers.
- There are more opportunities out there to deliver more value (and charge for it) to customers.
- Viewing your business from the customer's perspective opens up new ideas for additional services.

Considering the newly defined competitors, what else can you borrow from their world and product set—and add to yours—to create competitive advantage? Since you and your competitors all follow the same operations-based thinking, you can only look at each other for inspiration and ideas. Now that you define your business from the customer's perspective, you can actually take what is regarded as common sense in one market and apply it to *your* market to create a rule-breaking strategy.

You may want to repeat these two exercises with peers and customers to ensure that you grasp the full view of the customer. This will also help you identify new possibilities for products and services to delight customers and help you to create amazing experiences that result in the *wow* effect, positive memories, and a high impact on the business. It's all in the experiences.

REENGINEERING THE EXPERIENCE GUIDELINES
Dual Approach

To reengineer your customer experience, you need to work along two parallel lines. The first one is understanding, mapping, and fixing your current experience and its components. This effort will ensure a solid foundation, and the imagination and surprising effort required will add brand new aspects to the experience that will surprise and delight your customers. Without the right foundation, no surprise factor will work, and without the surprise factor, the experience will merely be okay. Remember, okay does not command a premium or a preference. Each effort complements the next to create a total customer experience with an impact.

The dual approach required to design customer-centric strategies is detailed in Exhibit 4.9. The diagram details the bottom-up efforts including

Exhibit 4.9   Reengineering Stages

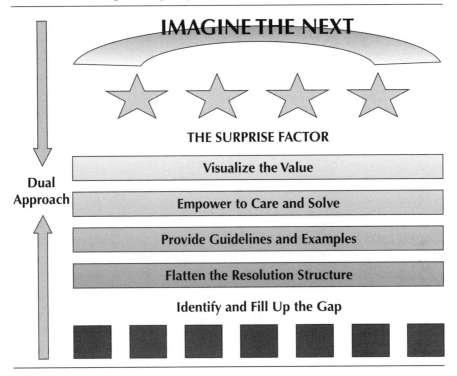

the process gaps and complaints resolution process and evolves all the way to the top—redesignng and reimagining the next level of experiences and relationships.

Reengineering Stages

Complementing the efforts detailed in the previous section, the following steps should be taken to support and guide the dual efforts detailed in Exhibit 4.9:

> *Step 1.*   *Touch Point Analysis.* The first step in experience recreation, a touch point analysis, is about mapping all the aspects of the company that the customer touches, directly or indirectly. From products to service people, channel distribution and web site, every touch point contributes positively or negatively to the total experience. Each touch point must be mapped and clearly defined to recognize its contribution to the total experience.

Step 2. *Customer Study.* A customer study is performed to learn what customers think about the different touch points and to allow customers to rank them in importance, need for improvement, and overall criteria selection. We recommend that you conduct a similar study with employees. Our experience has demonstrated serious gaps between what employees and customers regard as "must-have" features. These gaps result in misdirection of effort and frustrated customers.

Step 3. *Reprioritize and Fill in the Gaps.* The different touch points need to be reengineered to conduct the experience according to the criteria that the customers defined as important. The gap-filling process is designed to ensure that we deliver according to customer expectations and not ours. This work of perfecting process and experience is needed to build a seamless system that requires the least from the customer. During this stage, you may need to redevelop some processes, acquire some new tools to see the complete view of the customer, and add learning modules to allow your employees to understand your objectives.

Step 4. *Flattening the Resolution.* To ensure customer alignment, exceptions need to be factored into the reengineering process. Reexamine your complaints and exceptions resolution process and ensure that it will allow a "one call, solve it all" resolution. This means that the first person getting the complaint can address it and get it taken care of immediately.

Step 5. *Human Touch.* Make sure to empower your people to add their personal touch to the experience. It is, after all, the human touch that creates the emotional bond with customers that later is translated into strong preference and loyalty. As you have seen from the Customer Experience Analysis, it is actually the human aspect of the experience that has strong sustaining power. Any product feature will eventually be matched by competitors. The human touch, however, is unique, because of its sincerity and personalization.

Step 6. *Visualizing Value.* Even though, so far, you have not done anything very special, you still need to make sure that special tools are developed to allow the customer to visualize the value provided through your perfected process and experience. It is your responsibility, not the customer's, to ensure that the customer sees the value you deliver. Many companies fail that test and thus fail to capture the customer's hearts and wallets.

Step 7. *Surprise Them.* Add something customers do not expect. Be generous and show your customers that this experience is just a building block to a long-term relationship. Give them something beyond their expectations. Always factor a surprise into your experience. It will carry great weight with your customers and will be appreciated.

Step 8. *Building the Next.* Always think about what else you can do for the customers. Never settle. Look at the customer experience map (Exhibit 4.8), tap into customer emotions and aspirations, and design your experience from that perspective. If you fully understand your real business from the customer's perspective, it will suggest new ways of viewing your own operation and new ideas for what else can be done to differentiate and create preference. By reviewing the competition list in the customer experience index, you will be able to see where else your customer would target his or her budget, not those that are directly competing with you, but those that are tapping into the same emotions. By understanding this concept well, you will be able to identify those competitors and then steal ideas from their industry and implement them in yours. Those ideas might be common practice in their industry but will become a competitive advantage in yours because of their lack of precedence.

POWER TO THE PEOPLE: THE DIFFICULT SHIFT

Once upon a time, several years ago, the corporate power and the weight of the value proposition resided at headquarters. A few selected executives dictated the customer value proposition of products. The rest of the organization was told to act as a delivery agent of the value proposition chosen by headquarters. The customer's role in the whole picture was to pay and be thankful. The power of the value was locked in those few executives who controlled the whole food chain. With the advent of the Internet, their power was diluted and there was a shift. Customers now associate value with the *service* they receive from people. They will pay a premium for better experiences delivered by passionate employees. This represents a shift in power from headquarters to the agents in the street. The agents may be salespeople, service professionals, or dealers. They now hold the power of the value proposition. Combined with customers, the company's value proposition is now the domain of agents, customers, and headquarters, three entities sharing power and defining—together—the value proposition.

This is a shift in power many companies refuse to accept or are reluctant to utilize. They often try to run the show by the old rules, hoping that a few cosmetic exercises will suffice and customers will not notice. The notion that the CEO is often less important than a $25,000-a-year customer service representative is not too appealing. But the power has shifted. In reality, the customer will never meet the CEO and the CEO means nothing to him or her. It is the person in the store or the customer service center that makes the decisions or lends a hand to help the customer. This is the person to whom the customer gives loyalty. The success of store brands versus the national brand is a testimony for that shift. Store brands such as Kirkland[2] from Costco (and others) are winning out over the national brands and taking market share not because they are cheaper but because the customers associate value with the person who serves them—which happens to be a Costco employee. They view the complete experience, which now belongs to Costco, because they have people in the store to serve customers. If that total experience is good, the customer will select the Costco brand over a national brand—a brand from which he or she never received any additional value or service. The fact that Costco people are on the store floor and Procter & Gamble people are not will make all the experience difference.

Companies will have to adapt to the new distribution of power. It is not their choice. It is dictated by the customer. Reluctance to accept it will not help any organization become more competitive or catch up to customer needs. The total value is now created by executives, agents, and customers. The question is not how to avoid this shift, as many companies still attempt to do; the challenge is how to share the power correctly and how to bring the customers into the fold and turn them into evangelists.

WHAT IS YOUR CORE EXPERIENCE?

When connecting to customers and trying to see the world through their eyes, you will discover untapped opportunities you are missing every day.

You can easily get out of the commoditization rat race, but only if you start creating and delivering delightful experiences.

Starbucks: A People Business Serving Coffee[3]

Although many restaurants are in the business of serving coffee, Starbucks is able to charge much more for each cup, because it is focusing on personalizing the service and adding quality that customers can appreciate—quality for which they are willing to pay a premium. The company has defined its business not as a coffee producer serving people, but as a people business serving coffee. It goes beyond the semantics to the core of their identity and key differentiators. Starbucks was able to succeed by providing a wider variety of options that allowed customers to customize their coffee. The wider variety of options was just the first step. When this was combined with personal service, they were able to capture the customers' loyalty. Regular customers who attend the same Starbucks branch often enjoy the fact that the employees remember their personal preferences and their names. In fact, as Starbucks' appeal grew, along with its target audience, new, up-and-coming competitors began raising the bar of the "coffee experience" by providing even better experiences to a much smaller, but dedicated, segment of premium-paying customers.

To cement these experiences, the company unleashed its human power. By focusing on their employees and providing extra benefits such as health-care insurance to part-time employees, it ensured their commitment to deliver the experiences according to plan. Starbucks focused on creating the organization that is suitable for the experiences for which they wanted to be known.

Customers of Starbucks did not just respond with preference. Recently the chain introduced a coffee card, which attracted over 7 million customers. The commitment of customers reached a level at which they were willing to buy coffee and merchandise *in advance* through this card. It was their overwhelming vote of confidence in the company's customer-centric experience.

"Banks have managed to make money scary, confusing and boring. In talking to customers, we have all been guilty of being patronizing and overbearing. Most of all banks have got in the way of customers and their money."[4] This is an excerpt from an official press release issued by Abbey National, a U.K. retail bank, quoting Luqman Arnold, the bank's CEO. The press announcement discussed the bank's new customer experience initiatives, which involved a return to focusing on its core customers and a reinvention of the banking experience. There is something very attractive and humble in the tone and message of the CEO. But the reality is rather different. Abbey National diversified too much and in doing so, neglected their core retail customers. In addition, Abbey National focused on short-term results to satisfy the stock market and lost relevance with its core stakeholders— retail customers. The new customer initiative is geared toward changing that and becoming more relevant to its core customers.

A similar experience makeover was attempted by Abbey's competitor NatWest. A new ad campaign was launched with new colors and slogan, but not much beyond that. NatWest treated customer experience as a cosmetics exercise only, avoiding any fundamental changes to the operations or core value proposition. They were hoping that the new ad campaign would mask it all and the customers would not notice. Within the first week, customers noticed. The NatWest campaign generated cynicism among customers and bad press. The reason was quite simple: the bank fell into the trap of believing that a smart ad campaign can compensate for a lack of genuine, valuable experience. No changes were made in the branches or the bank's web site to reflect the proclaimed new experiences. This is a common mistake, often driven by ad agencies seeking new revenue streams. They sell their clients quick cosmetic fixes to a strategic and operational problem.

In the case of Abbey National, which changed its name in the process to Abbey and also changed its logo and slogan, there are better chances of success because the bank looked deep inside its operation and made several important moves to change the total experience. Those changes included:

- New, easy-to-understand terminology replacing old jargon
- Redesigned communication and letters
- A new communication campaign
- 60,000 extra training days per year
- 600 extra people to service customers directly

"So we're starting a revolution with the aim of democratizing money— helping everyone, not just the privileged few, get on top of their money. In one sense this is just a return to our roots. Abbey began as a building society to help ordinary people buy land so that they could vote, because at the time only landowners were enfranchised" (from the same press release quoted above). Abbey has much greater chances for success than its competitor NatWest; it is just too bad that it reached the realization about the need for such fundamental change *only* after it had disposed of over $100 billion in non-core assets, such as mortgages, savings, and investments—the reasons why it strayed away from its core customers in the first place.

Remember that experiences are not a "nice to have" that we pepper on top of our products and services. This is not an exercise in coming up with a new advertising or branding campaign. The customers will call your bluff if you choose this route. Experiences are not another program for increasing quarterly revenues. Experiences are the core of what you do and who you are. They are the unique identity of your business, products, and people. If crafted well and designed to delight, experiences will be the reason people pay a premium for your products, develop a preference for your brand, increase the portion of their budget allocated to your services, and increase the permanence factor by staying longer with your company. Great experiences contribute directly to your top *and* bottom lines. They should be the reason you are not just surviving the game but winning it.

Your experience is the one aspect of the relationship you can control. You cannot determine for the customer whether he or she will enter into a relationship with you—that is the customer's choice. But you can put the best experience out there to attract the customer's attention and court him or her into a relationship. The experience is up to you. This is the essence of your choice. Do you want to continue in the downward spiral of commoditization, constantly seeking new ways to cut costs, or do you want to make the business grow by providing continuously better value to customers? This *is* the experience choice.

Endnotes

1. "In the Pink" (*Gentleman's Quarterly,* December 2003), p. 294.
2. Matthew Boyle, "Brand Killers" (New York: *Fortune,* August 11, 2003), p. 51.
3. Howard Schultz and Dori Jones Yang, "Pour Your Heart Into It: How Starbucks Built a Company One Cup at a Time" (Sunnyvale, CA: Hyperion).
4. Jane Croft, "Group That 'Lost the Plot' Details its Plans to Get Back on Track" (London: *Financial Times,* September 25, 2003), p. 27.

5

CRITICAL CHOICE 4:
WHAT CUSTOMERS DO WE NEGLECT?

When it comes to commercial relationships, it seems that the meaning of the term "relationships" is twisted, and common sense no longer applies. In personal relationships we know that the more people we befriend, the less time we will have to invest in the relationship. Thus, we conduct different types of relationships with different people.

There are those we will never talk to, as we have nothing in common. These are people who tend to annoy us. It is as if we have a negative chemistry with them. Any relationship with them will just cause aggravation, frustration, wasted time, or even loss of money—or all of the above. Then there are those with whom we can have brief, casual discussions, usually about nothing of importance. The weather, sports, and politics may be typical connecting points with these people, but usually nothing personal enters the conversation. Our relationship with such casual friends usually lasts for a short time and is motivated by convenience; such relationships are easily replaceable. Then come our real friends. These are the people with whom we share our intimate feelings and with whom we commit to real relationships, acting as if it will last forever. These friends are fewer. The amount of time and emotional commitment required is substantial. Ultimately, we have our loved ones. These are the most meaningful, commitment-driven relationships with the highest chance of longevity.

The relationship rule is quite simple: the deeper the relationship, the fewer people with whom we can entertain it. The shallower and shorter the relationship, the more people we can consider. There is a direct correlation between the amount of time, resources, and overall investment and the quality and longevity of the relationship. One cannot invest lightly and expect a deeper, longer lasting relationship.

These basic, common-sense rules, however, seem not to apply when it comes to commercial relationships, or that is what executives want to believe, at least. The commercial idea of a typical relationship is this: we can establish deep, long-lasting relationships with anyone who is willing to pay. Any customer willing to pay our price (or close to it) is a prime candidate for a long, deep relationship. It is wishful thinking, and most customers are not buying it. It is, in fact, the exact attitude that turns customers off. They know that such a relationship cannot be conducted with everyone. Customers have learned that any relationship that attempts to attract everyone in fact attracts no one.

I often say that companies are from Mars and customers are from Venus. A company's version of a relationship is quick, transactional, and profitable. Customers, however, are seeking long-term commitment before they are willing to open their wallets and bestow loyalty. Companies only talk about the long term when it comes to the customer's commitment, not to theirs. In response, customers, taught to be suspicious after so many disappointments, are sober and reluctant. This is another dimension of the inherent conflict discussed in the previous chapter.

Without proper selection of participants and investment in the relationship, no relationship will last for too long or command any kind of a preference or premium price. But companies still insist that they can reach the masses and build intimacy and loyalty at the same time. The fact that they can advertise to millions through mass media makes many executives blind to the very basic rules of relationships. They truly want to believe that just reaching the masses will turn all of them into deeply committed, long-lasting customers.

Let's examine this issue from another angle. Products that appeal to the masses and are consumed en masse share a few characteristics:

- They are readily available everywhere.
- They are produced by a large number of competitors.
- They are, relatively speaking, cheaper to acquire.
- No loyalty is attached to them.
- They are consumed in the same way by all types of customers.
- They are symbols of commoditization.

From air to water to basic food, the wider the audience, the less loyalty, premium, or preference you will get from customers. Paper, pencils, public transportation, toilet paper, electricity, and sewage are other examples of heavily commoditized, similarly used products and services. Customers treat them all as basic necessities and nothing more, and they associate commercial value accordingly.

Widely used products and services are subject to heavy competition and accelerated commoditization. It is simply the nature of the market. If they appeal to mass markets, they ought to adhere to the lowest price possible to reach all these mass customers. Abundant availability will automatically lower the value perception of the products or services and drive the price and customer commitment down. The customer will treat those products and services as easily replaceable and will avoid any commitment to a certain supplier. Premium pricing or long relationship requirements will be foreign to a mass market business model. The two cannot coexist.

In light of these basic facts of life, it is unclear why companies are still devotees of the cultural belief that "the more customers, the merrier," without any basic selection criteria for relationships.

This critical choice is a basic foundation stone for customer strategies and relationships. In fact, in our Customer Experience Management (CEM) study,[1] 42% of the participants claimed that their company takes any customer willing to pay. In business-to-business and service companies, the numbers are 72% and 69%, respectively. This was an alarming finding, especially in industries that are highly dependent on long-term relationships such as business services and business-to-business products.

If you do not know which customers to neglect, you will not be able to build proper relationships. You will end up with every customer who is willing to pay, and some who purchased at a discount after not being willing to pay full retail price. Thus you will end up with customers who inherently do not appreciate your value proposition. They might agree to purchase your products because of a pushy salesperson or a deep discount, but basically they should not be in a relationship with your company. There is no match between your value proposition and your price, and their views and wishes.

As a result, these customers will be inherently dissatisfied. This dissatisfaction will be quickly transformed into a constant demand for service and attention that will drain your resources. This demand will tie up your resources with unappreciative customers while preventing you from servicing well those customers who are inherently matched with your company's value proposition and experience. The customers you need to neglect are also affecting your bottom line, as they are more costly to obtain and maintain. Another bottom line impact of such customers is the damage caused to the right customers, who did not receive the service they paid for and rightfully deserved. These customers might take their business elsewhere, which would impact on your revenues.

When we ask companies which customers they neglect, they often answer "those who have no budget." This simplistic approach is at best shallow lip service that demonstrates the lack of a serious approach to the matter. It results in salespeople acting without guidelines and approaching the masses. These salespeople are chasing many undesirable customers and forcing them through tricks and discounts to join the company's customer base. In reality, they are populating the customer base with customers who are much better served by the competition. Think about it: if you know that a certain customer is unprofitable, wouldn't you prefer him or her to be on your competitor's customer list? Let him or her deplete your competitor's margins and resources, while you focus on the profitable customers.

Companies seeking to establish sustainable and profitable relationships must face this critical choice and clearly define the customers with whom they will not be doing business. If these choices are not addressed, the company will form too many relationships that have shaky foundations. Establishing a relationship with the wrong customers will lead to costly service and will upset legitimate customers, who are not getting the service they paid for and rightfully deserve. By not addressing this critical choice, companies risk both the business with the wrong customers and the business with the right customers.

CUSTOMER SELECTION GUIDELINES

Establishing a company–customer relationship based on mutual benefit and appreciation is critical to customer profitability and longevity. Mass marketing practices operate on the concept of selling more of the same to as many people as possible. The main leverage point of mass marketing is volume—the higher the volume, the higher the profits, period. Customization and personalization are counterintuitive and undesirable. Mass marketing attempts to reach as many customers as possible and convince them all that they need a certain product or service. That product or service is hardly differentiated from the competition and, in the eyes of the customers, does not deliver unique, personal value. Thus the customer quickly opts for a discounted product. It is a natural response to the company's economic approach to relationships. Customers simply reciprocate.

Customer-centric strategies, however, assume that every customer is unique and different. Their underlying promise is personalized or customized experience that goes beyond the product and creates perceived differentiation in the eye of the customer. Customer-centric companies are willing to bear the additional investment associated with personalization and unique experience, knowing very well that the right customers will appreciate it and be willing to pay for it. Thus they seek to target the customers most suitable to appreciate and be willing to pay a premium for their specific products or service.

The temptation to appeal to the mass market—in the name of maximizing revenues—leads many companies to target their products to a large pool of customers who are not right for their products. These customers, because of the inherent mismatch between themselves and the value sold, will not be happy or satisfied, even though they receive a level of service well beyond the price.

Choosing which customers we will work with and which ones we will reject is the cornerstone of establishing relationships with the right customers.

Samsung: Making the Tough Choice

When Samsung's Chairman and CEO, Kun-Hee Lee,[2] decided to shed the old image of his company's products and focus on innovation and design, he faced a tough decision. His products would not command premium price and appreciation as long as they were on the shelves of commodity retailers. He made a choice and decided to neglect the discount retailers in order to increase his product's margins. Samsung pulled all their products from Wal-Mart and Target and focused on the high-end stores. Without this courageous move, Samsung products would have never had a chance of making it to the high-end market. Mr. Lee knew that by pulling out of Wal-Mart and Target (i.e., undesired customers), he freed resources and made room for Samsung to delight and treat their core, desired customers. His decision paid off, both in recognition and in higher price points and margins for the products: in 2003, Samsung reported record revenues of $36.9 billion.

As part of its strategy, every company must define in detail the key factors that define a desirable versus an undesirable customer. Such definitions must be the guiding lights for the marketing and sales operations as they generate leads and qualify prospects. Customers who do not fit the guidelines must be neglected, because they represent not only a potential loss but also potential damage to other customers.

If you knew that every mismatched customer costs your company $2,500, would you even consider sending a salesperson on a $1,000 flight to try and close the deal? Absolutely not; lack of knowledge about customer profitability and the cost of service and complaints is one of the reasons companies fail to address this critical choice. They cannot define which customers to neglect because they lack some basic information. Without the information, they continue with the "pooling" method, assuming that one customer's losses are covered by another customer's profitability. Thus they think they do not need to manage profitability per customer or know where they lose money. In fact, the "pooling" method is a recipe to lose money via your profitable customers when you don't deliver the promised service and experience to them. It will also cause you to bleed money through customers who should be in your competition's customer base and cause the competitors to lose the money.

Establishing the financial benchmarks and analyzing the cost of customers, including annual value and lifetime value, are at the core of defining desirable and undesirable customers. They are the tools to make this critical choice.

CHARACTERISTICS OF DESIRABLE AND UNDESIRABLE CUSTOMERS

What is the profile of the customers most suitable for your organization's value proposition, products, and services?

Select one target customer segment and try to paint as detailed a picture as possible of your desired customers. Avoid confusing different customer segments and focus on one customer segment during this exercise to ensure clarity and maximum details. Consider the following characteristics of business-to-consumer (B2C) and business-to-business (B2B) segments while completing this activity:

B2C	B2B
Income level	Company's size
Demographics	Total budget
Hobbies	Global reach
Complementary products/services used	Company's margin
Social background	Role of product
Family status	Product's level of criticality
Occupation	Track record with vendors
TV preferences	Expected life of relationship
Outdoor preferences	Innovator or follower
Cost of service	Cost of service
Annual value	Annual value
Lifetime value	Lifetime value
Cost of selling	Cost of selling
Growth opportunities	Growth opportunities

Our desirable customer is _____

_____

_____

_____

_____

_____

_____

Is your proposed profile of the desired customers generic? Is it appealing to the masses or too few? Can you identify rules to weed out the wrong customers? Do you have sufficient measurements to identify these customers? These are some of the questions you should use to qualify your response to the above exercise.

What is the profile of the customers who are unsuitable for your organization's value proposition? Select one segment of unsuitable customers and try to paint as detailed a picture as possible of your unsuitable customers. Again, use the characteristics for B2B and B2C customers listed in the table above as your guide.

Our unsuitable customers are _____

_____

_____

_____

_____

_____

Does your proposed profile provide clear guidelines to salespeople? Does it weed out few customers or identify a group that is inherently unsuitable for your value proposition and price point? Can you see many customers fitting this profile in your current customer base? How did they get there?

Progressive Auto Insurance: Power of Focus

Peter Lewis, CEO of Progressive Auto Insurance, built his company on the undesirable customers of other insurance companies—the high-risk drivers. Progressive did not offer their services to all drivers, but only to the well-defined group of high-risk drivers. The company created a special offering for this segment, which allowed Progressive to charge a premium for that differentiated offering.

By knowing their desirable and undesirable customers, Progressive was able to build a very healthy and profitable company.

CUSTOMER ROLE

What is the role of the customer in an organization? When asked, many executives reply "to buy our products." How many? At what margin and for how long? What else do you want the customer to do for you? These questions usually cause the executives to squirm in their seats but often do not produce any better response than the original, vague statement.

Lack of customer role definition is the first symptom of a product-focused company. By not having a detailed, measurable definition of the desirable customer, companies are basically losing out on additional customer opportunities. The customer role is another dimension of the relationship definition. After selection of the right customers and neglecting the wrong customers, understanding your expectations from customers is crucial to maximizing the relationship's potential. The role of the customer provides detailed, measurable guidance on how the relationship will evolve. It sets the ground rules for relationships. It also ensures that the relationships will be maximized and no opportunity will be missed. The definition of the role of the customer is a natural follow-up to the selection process. It lets companies maximize their relationship potential with their desired customers. This maximization assists in compensating for the loss of the undesirable customers. The original selection also ensures that the company will have more resources available to dedicate itself fully to the relationship and maximize it.

The role of the customer is the blueprint for the relationship. It serves multiple purposes for marketing, sales, and customer service. Marketing should develop a complete plan to provide value for those customers, a plan that should encompass all the aspects of the relationship including cross-sell and up-sell, as well as a long-term selling plan. When launching lead-generation campaigns, marketing should focus on the right customers and weed out the undesirable customers. It should also set the right expectations with customers. Additionally, marketing may utilize the definition of the customer's role to establish references and success stories with customers as part of their role and responsibilities.

Sales should focus their efforts on establishing long-term relationships with clear milestones for additional business, based on achieving certain value successes with the customers. (Value success is the customer realization of full value for his or her investment in your products and services.) When focusing on the long term, sales cannot drop the customer after the initial sale, or hand them off to a lower-level account manager. The right salesperson must stay on board for the long haul to maximize the long-term opportunities. The customer role will ensure that the salesperson maximizes the relationship potential not only in the first purchase, but also over a longer period.

As for customer service, they too will have to adapt to the customer role definition. From identifying areas for cross-sell and up-sell to soliciting referrals, customer service must be tuned in to the customer's role and life cycle. But the most important aspect of their function is to ensure that the customer realizes value success so that the next stage of the relationship will be realized.

Imagine what happens when the selection criteria are not applied and the customers' role is not defined. Every day thousands of salespeople are chasing business without knowing whether it is good or bad business. (In fact, they do not care, as they are compensated based on new business development, regardless of its quality.) They bring in new business and often receive special bonuses for doing so. Every day, companies are paying bonuses for new customer sales that might be unprofitable. Every bonus paid now makes these losses even greater! Additionally, by not defining the customer's role, companies manage to obtain only a fraction of the maximum potential of the relationships. Leaving money on the table in the process, companies fail to maximize the potential and thus generate a much lower return on their sales investment. Companies are deepening their losses that result from unprofitable customers and unrealized relationship potential by not defining the role of the customer.

CUSTOMER JOB DESCRIPTION

Imagine that your customer works for you. Just like an employee, the customer will do what you tell him or her to do and be measured accordingly. Imagine that you can assign roles and responsibilities that you will expect him or her to live up to. This is the essence of defining your expectations from the relationship. This is—to our surprise—another critical aspect of customer relationships that is left vague and undefined.

Exhibit 5.1   Customer Job Description

Customer will _____

Responsibilities	Measurements	Comments

Use Exhibit 5.1 to assist you in mapping the customer job description. It is a critical exercise because by not detailing expectations from customers, we do not build an operational plan to obtain those expected results. The opportunities may hit us in the face, but we will still miss them because of a lack of planning. We all want profitable, long-term customers. What does it really mean in numbers? This is the purpose of the exercise. Consider that your customer works for you. What would a job description for the customer look like? As you detail your expectations and measurements, consider the following questions:

- What is the length of the relationship?
- How many purchases do you expect him or her to make?
- What is the monetary value of those purchases?
- What is the overall lifetime value of the customer?
- What is the annual value of the customer?
- What growth in annual value would you expect?
- How many referrals would you expect the customer to make?
- What kind of insight would you expect? At what frequency?
- What other products or services would you expect to cross-sell?

Customer relationships may entail multiple responsibilities such as:

- *Purchase.* Define the optimal purchase size and value.
- *Repeat.* Repeat purchasing behavior.

- *Increase Frequency.* Increase frequency of purchases.

- *Evangelize.* Share his or her enthusiasm for your company with his friends and family.

- *Recommend.* Provide recommendations to others as part of reference program.

- *Provide Referrals.* Deliver names of potential customers.

- *Consult.* Provide meaningful insights to improve the experience.

- *Timely Payment.* Submit payment on a timely basis to avoid unnecessary and costly delays.

- *Forgive.* Mistakes happen, as we are all human. Forgiving our mistakes would be nice.

- *Larger Portion of Budget.* Dedicate a larger portion of your dedicated budget to the company's products as opposed to the competitors.

- *Upgrade.* Move up the experiences food chain to the next level.

- *Stay Longer.* Commit to our products for a longer period.

- *Support Margin.* Purchase products at a profitable margin.

- *Maximum Portion.* Dedicate the largest portion of your budget to our products.

All these examples can be clearly measured and attributed to customers. Most companies fail to go beyond the purchase and perhaps the repeat purchase aspects. They fail to see the fuller potential of the customer relationship. By defining all of the above aspects well, we can put in place an operational plan that encourages this behavior and rewards it to reinforce it. Without these details, we have marketing and sales resources being wasted, as we are shooting in the dark and missing under-the-nose opportunities. If we structure for referrals we will get them. If not, they will not come.

Review your responses to the Customer Job Description exercise. Did your definition include all of the possible responsibilities listed above? If not, add them to your list. Create a complete definition of customer roles and responsibilities that can then be translated into an action plan.

COMPANY'S JOB DESCRIPTION

In one of our seminars, a participant (we will call him John) defined one of the customer responsibilities as dedicating 85% of the customer's budget to his company's services. He basically wanted to be the primary supplier to the customers. This is an example of a well-defined, measurable responsibility/ expectation. Since many of the other participants in the seminar were customers of John's company, I turned to them and asked them "What would you demand in return for such high level of commitment?"

To John's surprise, his defined responsibility was not out of the question for his customers. They simply wanted the right level of commitment from his company to justify it.

All of the above aspects must be measurable so you can track your progress and ensure that you are reaching your business goals with your customers. As you go through this exercise, you will notice that you are asking a lot from your customers. Your competition is probably in a similar predicament. Ah, the moment of truth: every relationship must be mutual. You must then address the commitment you are willing to make to deserve the commitment level you are seeking from the customer.

For your expectations to be fulfilled, you must deliver on and exceed customer expectations. You must define your company's commitment to customers and the level of service you are willing to deliver to obtain the expectations you defined.

What Is Your Company's Job Description?

Considering your customer job description responsibilities, what would your company be required to deliver to justify the level of commitment you've defined for customers?

The following questions should serve as guidelines to help you consider your commitment as an experience provider:

- What experiences do you promise to deliver?
- What service level do you commit to? Measure and detail.
- What listening mechanisms are you willing to deliver?
- What response rate to ideas are you willing to commit to?
- What problem resolution commitment are you willing to make?
- How would you provide preferred treatment to the best customers?
- How do you ensure consistency across multiple touch points?
- What surprises are you willing to deliver to keep the relationship exciting?
- How do you ensure overall experience level even during growth phases?

Upon answering these questions, you will be able to determine whether your expectations are reasonable and whether you are able to sustain the desired relationship by doing your part. These answers will determine for you whether the desired customers will actually cooperate with the role you've assigned to them. It will be a result of what you are willing to commit to the relationships. It is advisable to speak to customers about their expectations when addressing these questions. This will ensure that your commitment levels and expectations are acceptable and will win the customers' hearts and cooperation.

_____

_____

_____

_____

_____

_____

You may want to repeat this exercise with your customers to validate their expectations and discover some new ideas you might have missed.

As you face your expectations and those of your customers, you can now examine the relationships and ask yourself whether it makes sense to be in them. Do you have the right match with customers' expectations? If you do not, then there are two possible explanations:

1. You are trying to court customers who inherently do not appreciate your value proposition.
2. You are trying to skimp on your customers while expecting the world from them.

Either way, serious changes will have to take place to address this mismatch. Either you will have to approach the right customers and neglect the wrong ones, or you will have to adapt your experiences to match the customers you have, so that you meet and exceed their expectations. There is one sure thing in this picture: the status quo will not last for too long. Any mismatched relationship breeds dissatisfaction. Dissatisfaction causes customers to wonder why they are in the relationship and whether there is not a better alternative out there. They most likely will find better perceived or real alternatives. They are less likely to stay trapped in a mismatched relationship. A mismatched relationship is a recipe for competitors to come and take over your customers.

Lacking customer role definition is like lacking a structure for the relationships. It is also a way to confuse employees about what they are expected to deliver, and it does not maximize the business opportunities per customer. Any relationship in which expectations are not clear from the beginning is doomed to be short lived and disappointing.

It is time we follow common sense and act as if we are in relationships. There is no point in abusing the term or defaulting into wishful thinking when, deep down, we know better. We cannot be in a relationship with everyone. The more customers we serve, the less value we can deliver. The larger the pool of customers, the lower the perceived value of our products. By attempting to change the natural rules of relationships, it is companies, and not customers, who are accelerating the commoditization of their own products. "One size fits all" fits no one in particular. Customers will not be happy and delighted but merely accept it as the least of all evils.

Not making this choice means defaulting to old habits of chasing every customer possible. It is a form of choice, even though not the right one. By choosing to neglect undesirable customers, we are choosing to stay in a longer, more intimate relationship with desirable customers. It is the profitable choice, and it is critical to the company's performance and prospects.

Endnotes

1. CEM Annual Global Study by Strativity Group, Livingston, NJ.
2. Samsung Example—BW article *Business Week,* January 12, 2004, p. 65, Yun Jong Yong: Samsung.

6

CRITICAL CHOICE 5:
WHAT KIND OF RELATIONSHIPS
DO WE SEEK?

Experiences are the domain of companies. Relationships are what they share with customers. A company cannot assume relationships without permission. In addition, relationships will not exist without cooperation. It takes two to form a relationship.

But what kind of a relationship do we seek? In our experience, the gap between customers and companies makes relationships very difficult. Although both use the term "relationship," they interpret it very differently. I often like to say that customers are from Venus and companies are from Mars. The popular John Gray theory explores the fundamental differences between men and women. Gray believes that conflicts and misunderstandings arise between the sexes because women are focused on relationships and men are focused on actions and resolutions. On the basis of this theory, I would argue that companies are seeking quick, detached transactions, whereas customers are reluctant to invest until they see a long-term commitment. Having suffered great disappointment in previous relationships, customers are now, more than ever, demanding a long-term approach before they offer loyalty and commitment. Companies, being ever more challenged to produce short-term results, seek quick, transactional commitments with no long-term investment or commitment. They both use the same term, "relationships," but have conflicting perspectives on what it means.

Companies must decide what kind of relationships they seek. After that choice is made, the operational changes and means of customer communication should follow. Quick, efficient, self-serving relationships are a legitimate strategy, but do not expect the customers to reciprocate with long-term loyalty. They are most likely to reciprocate with their own self-serving, efficient relationships, checking prices each time and shopping at discount stores.

If the choice is made for the customer version of a long-term, mutually beneficial relationship, then companies will have to adjust their operation in order to earn it. Customer relationships are earned one experience at a time. These experiences act as building blocks. The more blocks we use in the foundation, the stronger the ultimate relationship. And the stronger the relationship, the greater the loyalty: they are interdependent.

SYMBIOSIS VERSUS COMPETITIVE RELATIONSHIPS

There is a typical trap that must be overcome when companies begin to define their customer–corporate relationships: companies find themselves in direct competition with their customers. Both customers and companies are targeting the same pot of gold, and each is fighting for its rightful share. Each wants to retain most of the pot and leave the other person with the least gold necessary.

The pot of gold we are referring to is, of course, the customer's money. In current short-term, adversarial relationships, the customers try to retain most of their money and pay the minimum necessary; companies try to charge the most they can. This competitive situation locks companies and customers in a zero-sum game with no win-win resolution.

As much as companies refuse to accept it, this is the nature of their current relationships. It is usually amplified by a competitive struggle for what will be included in the purchased product. Now customers and companies are switching positions. The customer wants the most for the least price, whereas companies want to deliver the least for the highest price. This competitive, zero-sum game dictates the nature of the relationship and the level of trust (usually shallow to nonexistent) that characterizes the future of the relationship.

But there is another way to consider the relationship: as a symbiosis rather than a competition. In a symbiotic relationship, customers and companies are on the same side, seeing eye to eye the value provided and price paid. They do not compete; instead, each side takes steps to build goodwill and trust. Each side volunteers a bit from their stronghold to create a better relationship. Symbiosis can occur when both sides are convinced that the other side is not hostile but has their best interest in mind. To build such a level of trust requires disciplined efforts across multiple dimensions of the relationships. We will detail those dimensions in the next section.

WHAT IS THE ESSENCE OF A CUSTOMER-DESIRED RELATIONSHIP?

The customer interpretation of a relationship will be very similar to the type of relationship they seek in their personal lives. These relationships will have several dimensions, including:

- Selectivity
- Generosity
- Trustworthiness
- Mutuality
- Passion
- Privilege
- Genuine caring
- Choice
- Interactivity
- Conversational
- Exchanges

Imagine that a relationship is like a bank account. The more deposits you make, the more withdrawals you will be allowed. And in this bank, there is no permission for overdraft, although short-term loans may be made. Each dimension is a way to make deposits in the relationship account with the customer. The more you make, the better your account performs. Let's examine each dimension and its meaning for corporations that made the critical choice to satisfy the customer's desired relationship.

Selectivity

In any relationship, the selectivity dimension is critical. If everyone is allowed in, it becomes diluted and less attractive. The greater the number of participants, the lower the common denominator of the participants and the less the relationship can address specific needs, wishes, and expectations. Often companies, in the name of market share, develop relationships with many customers who inherently should *not* be their customers. These are people who will never appreciate the value proposition and will create constant friction. Thus they will constantly express this friction in the form of complaints that require high maintenance. This high maintenance will come at the expense of the right customers.

A recent trial conducted by Progressive Insurance[1] could bring the concept of selectiveness to a higher level. The company offered drivers special computer chips that measure their driving habits and behavior. The chip records how far they go, their speed, and other factors. Those factors are then used to create a customized insurance policy based on the driver's own patterns. Drivers have a choice of reviewing the chip results and accepting or declining an insurance policy based on the results. Although the jury is still out on whether this concept will become accepted practice, it is clearly bringing personalization and selectiveness to a new level. The driver is no longer part of a geography or age group but rather is treated as a unique individual unlike anyone else.

Being selective is about communicating to customers that they are different, unique, and part of an elite group. It is also about dedicating more resources and attention to fewer relationship partners, rather than spreading yourself too thin with a few useless resources for too many customers.

Generosity

True relationships are characterized by the generosity of the partners. Customers pay a premium, even if a similar utilitarian service or product is available elsewhere. Companies provide beyond-expectations service that surprises customers. The key is not just to meet expectations, but to exceed them. We often confront clients who believe they do exceed expectations, only to hear their customers claiming that their best is not good enough. Also, what the company considers unique to itself has been available *free* from competitors for several years.

Generosity involves making an investment in the relationship and then delivering more than the basics in order to send a message of long-term commitment. A generous experience will be justified not by the current price paid for a one-time transaction but by the fact that it is a down payment on future purchases. Only companies that believe there will be such future purchases bother to make the investment. For the customer, this investment is an important signal of the company's intentions and plans for the future. Generosity reaffirms to the customer that the company shares the same definition of relationships. It builds a bridge of trust toward future loyalty.

When General Electric (GE)[2] was looking to forge stronger relationships with customers, they applied the generosity rule by offering customers something new: the company's legendary management practices. Going way beyond products and services, the company investigated the business challenges its customers were experiencing and then offered to send their internal experts on Six Sigma and process reengineering to help customers solve their problems. GE provided an additional, generous service that went beyond expectations, and in the process it scored highly with those customers, who were now in emotional debt to the company. They repaid the debt by purchasing more products and services from GE.

During a trip to India, I stayed at the Renaissance Mumbai Hotel and Convention Center. The hotel surprised me with a small touch of generosity I had not seen elsewhere. The touch was simple; it was chocolate. No, I do not mean the chocolate placed on the pillow every night during turn-down service. This little night-time chocolate, also known as "missing in action" to many business travelers, is usually a sign of corporate cost reduction efforts that have reached ridiculous levels. The night-time chocolate at the Mumbai Renaissance Hotel was accompanied by a bookmark with a kindly, insightful message. What impressed me more, however, was that each time a fax or a message was delivered to my room, it was accompanied by a small chocolate. Each time laundry was sent to my room, a little chocolate accompanied it. It was a small, not too costly, symbol of generosity, one that made me smile each time I received one (by the end of the trip, I had a large pile, but I was still impressed each time again). This little generous gesture made this hotel stand out in my mind. Generosity does not have to be expensive. It has to be thoughtful. For a hotel that prints its mission "Delighted to Serve," on every piece of paper, generosity comes naturally. After seeing this motto printed everywhere, I wondered why other companies do not put their commitments in writing and at high frequency. It could serve as a constant reminder to both employees and customers of the type of relationship the company is striving to deliver. At the Renaissance in Mumbai, the constant reminder in the form of printed message combined with the generous gesture of chocolate created a true differentiation and a commitment on my part to come back and to share the experience.

Trustworthiness

Trust is not a black-and-white matter, but rather a matter of degree. The greater the trust, the more commitment will be made to the relationship. Trust is built through actions and fulfillment of commitments made by the company. A promise of an on-time delivery, if kept, will become a trust-building factor. A commitment to a certain quality level or consistency of service will be another. The greater the trust, the more contributions are made to the relationships account.

Mutuality

Mutuality is greatly misunderstood. Companies think that by allowing the customer to pay for their products, they build mutuality into their relationships equation. This understanding belongs to the efficient, self-serving interpretation of relationships. Companies must find new ways to interact with customers and allow mutuality to flourish. The more actively involved the customer is, the more vested he or she will be in the relationship.

Mutuality is a way for companies to demonstrate actively that they are willing to partner with customers, rather than dictate to them what is good for them and how much they should pay for it. Building mutuality into the relationships equation will require rethinking of some basic value propositions of the company. But it will pay off and justify itself with greater loyalty and vested customers.

Passion

This dimension is clear when it comes to personal relationships but is often neglected when it comes to commercial relationships. Passion is a major magnet that attracts people. If you have passion in your company's DNA, customers will know; they will be attracted. People love to relate to passionate people and seek to be part of what they do. Nurturing passion in your people and company will go a long way toward creating a powerful glue that will keep your chosen customers actively involved in the relationships.

Co Op Bank in the United Kingdom[3] has taken an extra step to share its customer's passions. The bank regularly polls its customers on their social agenda and then lobbies lawmakers to support these agendas. By doing so, the bank shares its customers' passions and forges stronger relationships that last. The bank is no longer just a provider of financial services, but a partner in their customers' personal lives.

As attractive as passion is in a relationship, it is also difficult to create and sustain. Burdened with cynicism and corporate politics, it is a tough challenge to generate passion within the organization. It is exactly that challenge that makes big winners of the few companies that manage to create passionate organizations and passionate people. They are big winners in the battle for customer relationships.

Privilege

After the dating period, most couples tend to slip into inertia and take their loved ones for granted. A similar phenomenon exists in commercial relationships. After a honeymoon period, in which promises are exaggerated, expectations are heightened, and spirits are high, companies slump into maintenance mode. This really means that they take existing customers for granted and focus their efforts on new customers, repeating, of course, the same process of exaggerated promises and high spirits.

Companies that manage to nurture a sense of privileged relationships are the ones that give customers the feeling that it is an honor to be in a relationship with them. These are the companies that never left the dating, courting stage. They never plan to leave it, either. They keep the relationship fresh through innovative services and experiences and ensure that the customer feels desired every day. They deliver once-in-a-lifetime experiences every day. With such a compelling privilege, no customer in his or her right mind would look elsewhere. After all, why leave a privileged relationship for an unknown, risky relationship with someone else?

FAO Schwartz[4] failed in its attempt to deliver privileged relationships. After having been in a high-end position, the company decided to try to cash in on low-end customers. It placed stores in mainstream rather than high-end malls. Eventually its value proposition was diluted, and the premium customers no longer felt privileged. The low-end customers did not connect, because prices were still too high and they could go to the discounters. As a result, the company found itself in bankruptcy and was dissolved.

Although catering to the low end carries a short-term allure, losing the "privilege" aspect of the relationship often means losing the relationship altogether. When you try to be something to everyone, rather than something special for a select few, you end up meaning nothing to anyone.

Genuine Caring

Faking it is the biggest threat to any relationship. Lack of authenticity and genuine caring is guaranteed to place any relationship on the fast track to extinction. In their zeal to repeat their success, companies try to repeat their original experiences, often with lower quality people or materials. Very soon customers realize that what they are getting is a second-rate, pseudo-original experience that is not worth the price. Feeling cheated, they opt for a genuine experience elsewhere.

Customers are not interested in a copycat. They will not pay a premium price or give their loyalty to a fake version of the original. They may buy it, once, at a great discount (and they would still haggle). Genuine experience commands a real premium and contributes to loyalty and the relationship account. The genuine dimension sends a clear message of caring to the customers.

Choice

Customers do not like to be in a dead-end relationship with a "one size fits all" atmosphere. They want to know they are in the driver's seat, determining their choices and not having their choices determined by others. Thus the choice dimension plays an important role in communicating to customers the importance you place on relationships. Usually, companies that are not planning for long-term relationships do not invest in providing choice and selection. They try to minimize costs by minimizing selection and thus send a signal to the customer regarding their true intentions and plans.

Meeting growing competition from Seattle Coffee in the United States and Café Nero in the United Kingdom, among others, Starbucks[5] increased its options and choices to customers by launching a campaign called "Customize your cup." The goal was to allow each customer to feel that his or her choice was as unique and special as the customer was individually and that there was no one else in the world with this particular coffee combination. Through choice, the coffee became a personal expression, as individual as the drinker.

Choice delivers this individual feeling, which makes the relationship personal and intimate. As simple as it may sound, many companies fail to deliver and communicate the fact that customers have choices and thus a proactive role in the relationship. They perceive choice as a costly "efficiency buster." They fail to see the value of retaining customers for the long term, usually because their financial planning and customer role concept did not factor in such longevity. Choice will serve as a great contributor toward a long-term relationship by making a significant contribution to the relationship account.

Interactivity

Today's customers do not want to be passive recipients of your value proposition. They have more power today and they exercise it. The response to the variety of web sites that collect customer input, from Zagat.com to HotorNot.com, demonstrates the interest of customers in being active participants and making their opinions heard and acted on. (Just having their opinion heard no longer counts. Customers are tired of the old system, in which they send their opinions into a black hole that spits out generic thank-you letters.) You must build an interactive dimension into your overall value proposition to allow customers to contribute and participate in the creation of the value proposition.

The recent success of Apple iTune[6] and the recent trial of new Starbucks music cafes are both testimony to the need to incorporate interactivity into the value proposition to enhance the total value to customers. In the case of iTune, customers get a chance to download their preferred music and create a collection as unique as they are. The fact that no one's iTune collection is similar to anyone else's makes customers willing to join this already 3-million strong movement with over 85 million downloads and growing.

iTune appeals to technology-savvy customers. Many technophobic customers are reluctant to download their own music. This inclination does not mean that they do not seek a personalized, interactive music experience. Starbucks recognized this trend and created the Hear Music Coffeehouse.[7] Customers can interact with more than 150,000 songs from more than 20,000 albums; they create their own music CD with their own cover design, produced for them in less than 5 minutes. This new offering addresses the same need for interactivity and unique expression, while delivering it differently and in line with customer emotions (technophobic) and preferences (a latte).

Some would find this experience odd, as we make customers do the work (selecting and downloading) and yet charge them for it. We shift some of the traditional vendor's tasks to customers and yet charge the same price. But from a customer perspective it makes sense. Customers are trading the rigid, one-selection-fits-all approach that vendors often provide for a selection as unique and personalized as they are. And for that personal expression they are willing to labor *and* pay.

This personalized selection reinforces several other aspects of relationship, such as generosity (wide selection), choice (the customer chooses the music), and privilege (the relationship between the vendor and the customer is unique). Each collection reflects the customer's personal emotions, preferences, moods, and tastes.

When SAP, the German software company, wanted to introduce its new product line NetWeaver,[8] it turned to an ecosystem model to push it further and faster. Recognizing the influence of developers, it created the SAP Developer Network, a web-based collaboration and information tool that allowed developers from around the world to share ideas and concerns. The tool dramatically decreased the time required for the company to communicate with developers and customers. With more than 80,000 members, growth at a rate of 2,000 new participants a week, and 4,000 hits per day, this community is evolving into a powerful sales tool that is based on the relationship principles of transparency of information, personalization through the ability of each developer to address his or her own issues, and interactivity as the core of collaboration and privilege, as participants get the first look at new software and patches.

Creating this tool allowed the company to treat each customer differently while maintaining critical mass. It also allowed the company to accelerate adoption of its new product through developers who supported it and were empowered through the company's generous sharing of knowledge. By approaching the developers, who are influencers, the company inserted itself into the ecosystem of decisions and ensured that developers would not object to it but instead support it.

In fact, customers already *do* participate in creating your value proposition. They search the Internet and discuss the experiences you offer on web sites and in user groups in sessions over which you have no influence. They are active in recommending or dismissing products. As you read this chapter, hundreds if not thousands of customers are shaping your image and brand through web sites you cannot influence. If you accept this reality (which is not much of a choice for you), then you might as well embrace it and join it, rather than fight it. Proactively communicate with customers and build interactivity into your experience. Interactivity can be a major factor in customizing customer experiences or contributing to the experience's overall design. You may also consider facilitating customer-to-customer discussion. You can turn your customers into guides, coaches, and consultants.

Conversational

Are you ready to listen? Really listen? Listen with the intent to act? This is another critical dimension of relationships. Relationships in which one side refuses to listen are doomed to fail and dissolve quickly. Listening is not about an e-mail address for suggestions or an occasional customer satisfaction survey. A real conversation is a meaningful dialogue that you take up with the intention to learn and to act. It is an internal process ensuring that customer comments are taken seriously and that customers are regarded as partners in the creation of the total experience. When you achieve meaningful conversations, you can also achieve longer relationships. The longer you keep the conversation and the actions flowing, the better your relationships will be.

Exchanges

Exchanges are at the core of companies' expectations for relationships. Companies want to sell products and services. Unless they produce sales, none of the dimensions described here are commercially justified. The customer understands that fact as well. But what companies do not seem to understand is that they will not obtain exchanges (especially repeatable exchanges at good margins) without the rest of the relationship's dimensions. Exchanges are highly dependent on the generosity, passion, and trustworthiness of the experiences. Without these dimensions, there will be very little, if any, exchanges. However, the better the dimensions, the better the exchanges will be.

DIFFERENT RELATIONSHIPS WITH DIFFERENT PEOPLE

Customers differ in their needs, appreciation of value proposition, and willingness to work with you around your expected relationships. Your pool of customers represents all those who qualified to be your customers on the basis of our previous exercise. We are not discussing undesirable customers here. You need to design different experiences and relationships to ensure profitability for the company and suitability to customer expectations, standards, and wishes.

At this stage, we will examine customer segmentation in the existing customer base. From the perspective of a product or service strategy, all customers are treated the same way; companies seek to maximize revenues by minimizing customization. Customers are merely purchasers of the same product or service. They all pay the same price and are treated the same way. But from their own perspective, customers are completely different. For example, a leisure traveler relates to a hotel room and perceives its value completely differently than a business traveler does.

In the last few years, we have seen an accelerated commoditization of products and services. Customers today are treated to "one transaction fits all" and expected to love it and pay a premium for it. Multiple competitive and price pressures caused companies to skimp on the total value proposition by reducing the quality of ingredients or the number of service people available to provide for and delight the customers. The customers, of course, pay the price through longer hold times at the call centers, more indifferent staff in retail stores, and lower quality products. The gap between customers and companies is growing.

At the core of this gap is the desire to commoditize the customers and deliver the same solution to all. There is a widespread corporate myth that says "if we deliver the same to all, we capitalize on economies of scale." This myth leads many organizations to attempt—repeatedly—to deliver the same to all and hope that each customer will find in such bland experiences a personalized touch that will justify the price. What a fallacy! Talk about wishful thinking!

Companies must realize that "one size fits all" means "one size fits no one." Customers are applying their own version of "economies of scale" and opting for cheaper versions every time. In response, companies are seeking to reduce their costs even further, attempting to meet the customer's even lower price expectations. The result? Even lower quality products, fewer service people, more indifferent retail people, and so the story goes. The ultimate Catch 22, and no one is satisfied.

The cure requires understanding the different expectations of different customers and delivering different experiences in turn. No, it is not more expensive. The expensive way is to commoditize all customers and reduce them to the lowest common denominator. This carries a price tag that most companies refuse to measure: higher churn rate of customers, lower employee morale, and ever decreasing margins.

By designing different services for different customers, we are in effect matching the customer's preferred price points with the right service. At the same time we avoid the pitfalls of poor customer selection: overservicing customers who are willing to pay little and underservicing our top customers, who pay us handsomely. The current model, in which all customers are queued in the same line to the customer service center, does exactly that. There is nothing more upsetting to a top customer than being relegated to wait in line with customers who have not delivered top revenue. It is an insult to his or her commitment to the company. Such treatment will eventually force customers to revolt and take their business elsewhere. By refusing to recognize their uniqueness, we are forcing our customers into the hands of the competition, as they pursue the personalized, respectable relationship.

Customer segmentation allows organizations to differentiate their value proposition and deliver different experiences to different customers. It allows companies to develop customized sales and relationship strategies and to maximize the revenues per customer as a result. In addition, employees must understand customer segmentation in order to deliver the right services to the right customers.

Customer segmentation criteria differ according to your business, products, and delivered experiences. Segmentation criteria might include:

- Variety of products used
- Customer's business
- Customer lifestyle
- Customer consumption habits
- Order/deal size
- Frequency

- Last sale
- Profitability
- Customer's influence on other purchasers
- Margins
- Relationship longevity
- Annual value
- Lifetime value

SEGMENTATION CRITERIA

List the relevant customer segmentation criteria for your organization.

1. _____

2. _____

3. _____

4. _____

5. _____

Exhibit 6.1   Customer Segmentation

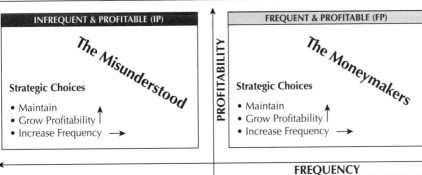

Exhibit 6.1 is an example of a customer segmentation mapping exercise that allows organizations to categorize their current customer base, which is critical for understanding which customers deliver the revenues and profits and for designing strategies to increase those customers. At the same time, customers who cost the company, because of high maintenance costs, need to be managed with a certain strategy: either change the delivered experience to make it profitable or let them go to the competitors. Other alternatives include customer tiers such as Basic, Silver, Gold, and Platinum levels. Each customer is mapped to the right level and receives a different service level according to status.

The Moneymakers

The moneymakers are the customers who deliver the healthiest margins; they should constitute the bulk of your business. They are the ones who are high on your frequency and profitability charts; they conduct business with you frequently and deliver healthy revenues and margins. (Beware of the revenues-only measure, however: often the highest revenue customers are thin on margins, if not actually unprofitable, because of heavy discounting.) Your moneymakers are the only ones about whom you can say "the customer is king." They are the reason you are in business. You must design an experience that justifies their loyalty. They must feel you are giving them generosity, choice, and interactivity. After you have designed a preferred experience, you can work on strategies to increase frequency and profitability. Ensuring that your investment is a special experience for them will pay off for you.

The Misunderstood

The misunderstood are the customers with low frequency but still high profitability. Their infrequency, because of consumption differences or simply different needs and lifestyles, blinds you into believing they lack loyalty or are not worth the effort. In fact, they can be quite profitable, and they deserve your special attention. Do not force them to move to the Moneymakers quadrant. (Some may be willing to, but others may simply not fit the definition.) They might already be delivering all they can. But nurture the relationships and be on the lookout for additional services you can sell them to provide a more complete experience. In any event, do not do so *before* you ensure that you deliver a differentiated service that recognizes their positive and welcome contribution to your business. Make them feel wanted and privileged, and *then* expand your business with them.

The Candidates

The candidates are those customers who disturb your business and make it less profitable. They do so both by costing you directly (by abusing your service and maintenance resources) and being unprofitable. But they also drive additional costs. They are drawing resources away from the moneymakers and the misunderstood. Their high maintenance cost (especially in light of the revenues they deliver) is a dual loss impact for you.

Why are they even with you, you may wonder? There are a few reasons. They may have bought from you originally through aggressive sales campaigns that promoted market share expansion at all costs. They might be the fruits of desperate salespeople trying to close on any new customer at any cost. They might be respondents to your desperate, end-of-quarter attempt to catch up with the quota. In any case, they do not belong in your customer base. You need to move them to another quadrant or move them out. Every day they constitute dual cost impacts and affect the service level of your best customers, the moneymakers.

If you fail in moving them up to a better quadrant, then move them to the competition. There is nothing sweeter than a dual win. You reduce your costs, and your competition gets entangled with expensive customers who will drain their resources and distract their business. This is a win-win situation. Free your time and resources to deal with and delight the moneymakers.

The Lost Souls

The lost souls are here because they have no other place to be. And you are the proud recipient of the costs associated with that confusion. Mass market advertising brought them here. They are not really willing to pay your prices, but they have gotten used to the lavish service you provide. They live at the moneymakers' expense and believe that no one gets hurt in the process. Do not get blind-sided by the low frequency. They still cost you money each time they contact you. They still drain resources from the moneymakers. Just like the candidates, if you cannot convert them up, convert them out. Let your competition baby-sit them and deal with their indecisive, money-losing, costly behavior.

The rule of thumb is that the smaller the customer group is, the better and more personalized the experience should be, and hence the longer and more profitable the relationship. If we need to address the masses through the lowest common denominators, then we will most likely end up with a bland, boring experience that, at best, will satisfy a basic need but definitely will not go beyond it to a relationship-building exercise. The most appealing products to the largest group of customers are usually the cheapest, most undifferentiated, and lowest margin products. Just consider air, water, and basic foods such as flour, sugar, and salt. The smaller the customer base, the better you can group them based on personal preferences and emotions and tailor experiences they will appreciate and perceive as beyond the basic needs.

Paychex: Profiting from Someone Else's Unprofitable Customers

Sometimes the unprofitable customers of one company can be highly profitable customers of another company. The key to that change is in designing a specific, different experience for those customers. This is exactly what Paychex,[9] the small business payroll company, did when they focused their business on the unprofitable customers of ADP, which were the small companies with less than 50 employees. They provided similar service but a different price structure that appealed to small businesses. The founder of Paychex realized that the under-50-employee businesses preferred to connect via the phone and did not require a sophisticated support system such as the one delivered by ADP. Thus he delivered a more cost-effective option, while managing their expectations to meet his price structure.

ADP, Paychex's largest competitor, wanted to force its high-end price structure on low-end customers; in the process, it lost them. These customers saw no value in the extras delivered by ADP and thus refused to pay the premium associated with its price. Since they did not see the value added to the high-end service, a discounting campaign by ADP to attract them would have not made any sense. At best, it would have resulted in inherently unappreciative customers who would have been served at the expense of the best ADP customers.

The solution that Paychex found was perfect: it did not try to force customers into a mold they did not fit, but instead designed a brand new experience for them based on their needs and issues. Creating a new design, an experience just for them, ensured that it would fit perfectly and resulted in over a billion dollars in new business—based on the unprofitable customers of another company.

By focusing on this customer segment, they created a customized experience for them and managed to turn them into profitable customers and build a successful company.

Royal Bank of Scotland[10] (RBS) uses this segmentation concept in its mergers and acquisitions. Unlike other financial services conglomerates, which rush to paint every newly acquired company with their name, logo, and style, RBS instead keeps their acquisitions separate and unique. Each bank retains its name, logo, and approach to business. RBS executives actually allow two of their banks to have branches on the same street, opposing and competing with each other. They believe that different customers have different needs and that these unique needs will be fulfilled by one of their banks. By keeping the banks separate, RBS allows them to build unique identities and experiences, maximizing the market reach and penetration. Banks that insist on a unified look and style are actually trying to force their customers into a one-size-fits-all model, which usually causes customers to go elsewhere, somewhere their individuality will be respected and where they will not be asked to fit into a mold.

TAILORING THE CUSTOMER'S EXPERIENCE

As discussed before, customer segmentation is the key to providing maximum value to customers and maximizing revenues and margins. The process of tailoring the experience comes after segmentation. Recognizing that not all customers are created equal, nor do they ask for equal value or offer to pay equally, you must develop tailored experiences for each customer segment to suit the needs of that segment.

Tailoring is not about taking your high-end product, dropping a few features, and claiming that you tailored the solution for discount customers. This is the trap most companies fall into, another variation of forcing customers into a one-size-fits-all mold. It is another attempt to leverage economies of scale and expect the customers to adapt accordingly.

Designing experience is just like a bespoke tailoring service. It is about measuring your customer and fitting the experience to his or her size. It is about understanding that each customer group is unique, with its own needs, hopes, and dreams, and then creating an experience that fits those emotions. These experiences will differ in the product sold, the additional services wrapped around the product, and the price point for the product.

When you are tailoring relationships to customers based on segmentation, it is crucial that you provide both pleasure to the customers and profit to the company. Both customers and company need to win in the relationship. If the desired customer experience is not profitable to the company, you should not be serving this customer base. If you cannot find a business model that will lead to profitability, do not fall prey to market share considerations, but simply let the customer go.

If your margins do not allow you to deliver a truly delightful experience, that is another signal to let go of the customer. The tailoring process must be set up to ensure that each customer segment receives the value for which it pays. This means that each segment's experience is different across multiple aspects—the actual product, the services provided, the level of intimacy and customization, and the price point charged. You will not succeed in faking an experience. There is no point in trying. And delivering a commoditized experience is also out of the question, as it will hardly prolong the inevitable: your customer defecting to a competitor.

So the tailoring process must pass both rules at the same time—be pleasing to the customers and profitable to the company.

One of the common mistakes we encounter is the failure of companies to understand their cost structure. The company cannot tell whether an experience is profitable or not. It cannot measure the consequences of its plans accurately. Old practices of economies of scale and one-size-fits-all lead to "allocation"-based assessment and other inaccurate analyses. If you fall within this category, it is time to develop new skills and tools. There is no point in segmenting and tailoring experiences if we cannot figure out whether they are contributing to or damaging the company's bottom line. No excuses such as "we are making it on volume" or "overall we are doing well" are sufficient. This is exactly the attitude that leads you straight into the hands of the candidates and the lost souls and damage your value to the money-makers and the misunderstood. It is tempting to speak in generalities, but they will lead you away from the truth. Get your numbers clear and accurate, and the truth will set you free (from the wrong customers and unprofitable behavior, that is).

Virgin Wireless: The Art of Focusing

When launching their service in the United States, Virgin Wireless[11] made a tough choice not to sell to every customer out there. They decided which customers to neglect, and they decided to focus on teenagers and singles in their early 20s. This focus gave the company a powerful advantage, as it was able to customize service just for these customers. The company's phones were equipped with several teenager/singles-style features like a special blind date button. This feature allows customers who are stuck in a miserable blind date to press the button. The button will turn on the phone and make it sound like a call is coming in. The customer can then apologize, use the call as an excuse to cut the date short, and end his or her misery.

If Virgin Wireless had been appealing to the masses, such a button would not have been relevant, and most customers would have rejected it. By focusing on a well-defined segment and understanding their emotions and aspirations, the company was able to create a tailored experience so successful that the company generated 1 million new subscribers in its first year in the United States.

American Express: Profiting from Variety

American Express[12] provides financial services primarily in the form of credit cards. The company, however, adapted its experience to each customer segment and wrapped it with additional services and prices to match the desired experiences:

- Green Card with Rewards Program is for the mainstream customer who seeks free gifts.
- Small Businesses are linked to the Open Network, which is a referrals and services network of many other small businesses. These customers also receive valuable expenses management services.
- Corporate Charge Card allows companies to manage their expenses across thousands of employees.
- Black Card targets the super rich who are willing to pay a significant premium to be recognized. This is a by-invitation-only card.
- Platinum Card attracts the wealthy customer who is seeking Luxury Service, and American Express delivers *Departures*—a high-end, topical special magazine—and discounts to leading hotels around the world, as well as concierge services.
- Blue Card is for the cost-conscious customer who is seeking refunds up to 5%.
- Rewards Cards offer incentive programs for corporations via prepaid cards.

Each of these cards delivers basic credit services, but each is priced separately and delivered with completely different experiences and price points. This way American Express ensures that every experience is profitable and relevant to each customer segment.

By tailoring the experiences and making sure that no experience will touch the others, they live up to the promise of treating different customers differently and getting away with charging different rates for it. In an environment of tough competition with Visa and MasterCard, when the average credit card brings in about $55 as an annual fee, American Express often gets away with $300 or more. The key to this success is segmentation and different treatment of different customers.

Relationships are delicate and vulnerable. Companies, like individuals, must select them carefully and nurture them. One simple, stupid move can destroy years of investment. As companies evaluate the type of relationships they seek with their customers, they ought to demonstrate serious investment and commitment if they expect similar response from their customers. Every type and level of commitment will encounter a similar response from customers. The relationships will be mutual and draw equal efforts from customers. It is foolish to believe that companies can form millions of shallow relationships and yet expect that customers will be deeply involved. Just as this line of thinking does not work in personal relations, it is doomed to fail in commercial relationships.

As relationships are nurtured, the level of the company's commitment is also judged by the completeness of the approach. Covering all bases to ensure that the relationship is personalized, generous, and interactive will go a long way toward generating a similar commitment from the customer. The choice of the type and level of relationship commitment is a serious one facing every company. Twisting the natural laws of relationships will not suffice, and it will not substitute for the tough choice, a choice that requires a courageous response. Because of years of corporate behavior that twists the laws of relationships, it is easy to invest minimally in the relationship and at the same time expect a greater return from the customer. It has been wishful thinking for years. It takes courage to face the truth and start swimming against the current. But the rewards for those who make this choice are worth the effort.

Endnotes

1. "Can Progressive Stay In Gear?" (New York: *Business Week,* August 9, 2004), p. 44.
2. Diane Brady, "Will Jeff Immelt's New Push Pay off for GE?" (New York: *Business Week,* October 13, 2003), p. 94.
3. "Banking on Ethics" (New York: *Business Life,* November 2003), p. 20.
4. Queena Sook Kim, "Storied FAO Is Casualty of Tough Holiday Toy-Pricing War" (New York: *Wall Street Journal,* December 3, 2003), p. B1.
5. Alison Overholt, "Listening to Starbucks" (*Fast Company,* July 2004), p. 50.
6. Pui-Wing Tam and Sarah McBride, "Has Jobs Gone Hollywood?" (New York: *Wall Street Journal,* Monday, June 14, 2004), p. B1.
7. Ibid., Overholt.
8. *www.sap.com.*
9. *www.paychex.com.*

10. Erik Portanger, "Royal Bank of Scotland Makes a Name for Itself by Keeping Low Profile" (Brussels: *Wall Street Journal Europe,* September 23, 2003), p. 1.

11. Gerry Khermouch and Catherine Yang, "Richard Branson: Winning Virgin Territory" (New York: *Business Week,* December 22, 2003), p. 45.

12. *www.americanexpress.com.*

7

CRITICAL CHOICE 6: HOW DO WE CHANGE OUR ORGANIZATION TO AVOID THE SILO-BASED CUSTOMER TRAP? HOW DO WE ASSUME COMPLETE CUSTOMER RESPONSIBILITY?

So who owns the customer? "Everyone" is the common answer. "We all own the customer. We all bear the responsibility to delight the customer and ensure their satisfaction," people say. I love it when they say it—another corporate fallacy with no support, noncredible and useless. "So, if your top five customers depart," I counter, "who will get fired?" At this point, the executives are looking around with a puzzled expression, knowing quite well the statement was hollow. They quickly realize that the gap between slogans and reality is too large to bridge.

MANAGING ACROSS ALL TOUCH POINTS

Every time customers engage with a company, they come across multiple functions that represent multiple touch points. From a customer perspective, all these touch points and interactions represent the company and create or contribute to the overall customer experience. The popular perception would have it that sales or marketing is responsible for the customer. In reality, everyone is responsible for the customer. Every aspect of the business impacts on the customer experience positively or negatively. Every function makes a contribution to the total value delivered. This simple truth is often lost in many companies, which tend to assume that customer responsibility is delegated to a few select areas alone. When one examines the organizational choice regarding customer experiences and relationships, it is important to take a look at the complete picture of employee and organizational responsibilities. It is necessary to examine the touch points and see how far and how deep the customer goes in his or her interaction with the company. Identifying those touch points will allow us to understand better the need for an organization-wide approach to customer relationships. It will also help in designing a better organization to deliver the desired experiences and relationships.

Over the course of the company–customer relationship, customers and organizations come into contact in multiple ways: web site, brochures, initial inquiry, point of purchase, contract, shipping, customers' manuals, customer service, returns, and so on. A common mistake made by many companies is to develop the marketing and sales touch points, make them customer focused, and neglect the others. This mistake creates a significant gap between the promise to the customer and the ultimate delivery. Well-developed sales and marketing campaigns heighten the customers' expectations, only to create greater customer disappointment. Every touch point creates an experience and contributes (positively or negatively) to the overall company–customer relationship.

For example, what is the impact of accounting on your overall customer experience? How does operations impact your customers? What is the legal department's responsibility? Are the shipping people trained on how to service customers? Understanding the full scope of your company's touch points is a first step toward building an organization that can create the right experience for the right customers and develop lasting company–customer relationships.

TOUCH POINTS ANALYSIS MAPPING

Map all the people/functions that touch or impact your customers' experience and identify the specific roles/people that actually make the impact. Note that often, some of the touch points are not reporting to/employed by your company but they are still making an impact on your behalf. Dealers, outsourcing suppliers, and shipping companies might not be under your direct control, but from a customer perspective, they are extended parts of your organization. Their behavior and quality of service directly impact on the perception of value delivered by your company. Make sure to include all of them in the analysis.

In Exhibit 7.1 list all the functions, and then in the Touch Point column, describe the way they touch customers. Follow the description with a listing of who exactly is delivering this service. Finish the exercise by ranking the

Exhibit 7.1 Touch Points Analysis

Function	Touch Point	Delivered By	Experience Quality

quality of experience each function delivers. When ranking experience quality, be honest with yourself. If you are not sure, refer back to customer satisfaction surveys or customer complaints. They are likely to paint a vivid picture for you. You may score the experience quality from 1 to 10, with 10 being the highest, most satisfying experience. Ultimately, the weakest link in the touch points mapping, which is the function or touch point that scored the lowest, is the touch point that determines the overall customer perception of the customer experience.

Exhibit 7.1 is a quick reminder of the myriad functions facing the customers and touching them in one way or another. Without complete ownership of the customer and full enterprise engagement, the customer experience is doomed to fail.

This is another critical choice most companies prefer to avoid or simply ignore. After some tough choices on customer selection and experience definition, they often want to believe that change can happen without touching the organization. This flawed thinking costs many organizations the success of their customer strategies. Failing to understand the required organizational changes and addressing them immediately will result in several problems:

- *Misalignment of Processes.* Although you intend to refocus efforts on customers, existing processes may reinforce a contrary behavior in which efficiency and mass productivity will be rewarded and customization of service will be penalized. Conflicting processes are becoming common. Companies are trying to address both customer needs and their own efficiency needs—which are in conflict from the outset. Employees are often given inspiring slogans about the importance of caring for customers, but also harsh processes that conflict with customer-centric behavior. Confused employees are not sure about the company's real intentions. Ultimately, left with no other choice, employees will follow not the slogans but the money trail, which means employees will continue to do what they are paid for, despite all the great new slogans posted all over their cubical.

- *Credibility Challenges.* If you are like many other companies (and most likely you are, despite your attempts to believe otherwise), you have been there before. You've told your people about the need to focus on customers and fulfill their wishes. If your employees are like other employees, and most likely they are, they have developed a numb spot in their brain for those messages. They have been there before many times and seen that these declarations never materialize into any actionable, long-term commitment. Your employees have been there when great intentions were sent to the graveyard in the name of "we must close the quarter" or "we must close every deal"—rushed initiatives in which, again, we took money from anyone who was willing to pay, not counting the long-term implications for our best customers. After a while, the employees get the message. There are the nice, well-intended slogans, but then there are the realities. They let the nice slogans fade quietly, while continuing to do what they always did. They have developed a system to ignore these "program du jour" announcements. "This too shall pass," they say to themselves and each other.

- *Organizational Conflict.* You demand complete ownership and responsibility for the customer. You say you want to have a complete view of the customer, yet you are organized via a silo-based chart that forces the members of each function to care only about their small portion of the customer. Unless the organizational structure supports the new, customer-centric initiative, it is more likely to conflict with it, causing confusion and noncompliance. If there is no complete ownership of the customer, then sales will continue to care for their part, making impossible promises to get the deal closed and then throwing it over the fence to customer service to deal with the consequences. Meanwhile, accounting will continue to send inaccurate, irritating invoices, while shipping will miss shipment deadlines. This vicious cycle will be broken when the organizational structure is realigned to support the new customer strategy. Changing the organization to meet complete customer responsibility is inevitable.

- *Permission to Ignore.* The customer is the business of sales or service, not my problem. This common perception prevails in many organizations. The customer is the primary concern of a few functions, while the rest are not involved. Unless there is enterprise-wide engagement, it is easy for people and even entire departments to assume they are not responsible. They take on a role of back-end support and do not see the impact of their actions, or often misdeeds, on the customer's total value proposition. When a message is sent to everyone, just like an e-mail with a large distribution, everyone assumes it is someone else's job. They always assume they were merely notified, but not asked to act. The same thing happens when a customer-centric strategy is launched. Everyone reads the memo, but few, if any, take charge and start acting. Everyone assumes they were merely notified. The responsibility is someone else's. This is the ultimate permission to ignore.

- *Changing Attitudes.* The changes we are suggesting are not about structures and processes alone. People execute processes. People breathe life into organizations and their vision. Unless employees buy into the new vision and plan, they will not cooperate. Changing employee attitudes is the hardest part of any new way of doing business. It is not equal to changing processes. Issuing new guidelines will not be sufficient. Changing employee attitudes is a longer process than we estimate and requires diligence. Employees judge the seriousness of the customer strategy by the changes the company is willing to make to its operations. Employees are accustomed to measuring seriousness by the level of internal change. The deeper the change, the more convinced they are of the staying power of the plan. So in order to support employee attitude changes, make sure the message is delivered in a hard-coded way, through real changes and not just virtual memos. Then follow up diligently to demonstrate long-term commitment. Employees assign importance to actions, not intentions.

OBSESSION WITH TOOLS

All of the above issues are tough nuts to crack and require real effort. Many companies, driven by the short-term results mind set, are looking for shortcuts. Even though they know deep down there are no shortcuts to such major changes, eagerness is often more powerful than logic, so they find the answer—seemingly—in the form of tools. Companies are purchasing technology tools in the hopes that they will do the trick and prevent the need to do the hard work.

When they rush to invest in new customer-related technologies, avoiding the need to reexamine their relevant strategic and operational aspects, companies are fooling themselves into believing that technology cures everything, without the need to face the real challenges. At the same time they are setting up a guarantee for failure and wasted money and resources.

Some technology companies have played along. They have justified their products by claiming strategic capabilities and made much more outrageous claims than their technologies can actually deliver. Technology can never deliver excellent service to customers. Only people can. Technology products are merely a tool, operated by people. People determine the type, breadth, and quality level of the service they are willing to deliver.

Waving some fancy return on investment (ROI) analysis in front of the customers, technology companies rush to close the deal on the promise of great measurable benefits, fast. Even while signing the contract, they are busy with the next client, leaving their existing clients to figure out on their own what they have just got themselves into. As a customer told me once, "technology is a tool and even a fool with a tool is just a fool." I would dare to rephrase it by saying "a fool with a tool is an even greater and more dangerous fool." He believes that he possesses the solution and rushes to implement it, while neglecting to face the real challenges: changing people and processes.

Purchasing technologies and other tools is a convenient way to create shortcuts, a way to believe that one can check off the "customer initiative" item on a long to-do list, without the need to address the hard-core issues of organizational change and adaptation. In reality, if the customer initiative is a to-do list item, then you have missed the whole point. This is exactly why companies fail, because they fail to recognize that the customer is not an initiative and that satisfying customers is not about a piece of technology. The customer is not one item in a long to-do list. The customer should be the *whole* to-do list. It is either the core of the business and everyone is aligned with it, or it is not part of the core competencies of the organization.

Technology, however, has significant potential to improve the customer value proposition and service delivery. If aligned properly with a strategy, it can enhance execution and make it effective. Technology tools have advanced customer strategies and improved their results, but they have never addressed the complete picture of people, strategy, and processes—they never meant to do so, either. This responsibility always belonged to the executives. And no technology purchase can eliminate it. Despite the exaggerated expectations and sometimes exaggerated vendor claims, companies must realize that the tools are merely tools and will not do your job for you. They may save you time, but they will not replace your job.

The obsession with tools must end if companies want to start taking their customer strategies seriously. Although potentially useful and beneficial, technology and tools can complement solid customer strategy, but they should never trigger it.

ORGANIZATION-FOCUSED CUSTOMER

As you look at your current organizational structure, you will probably see an organization with functional expertise arranged in groups. Thus sales activities are under one umbrella, shipping is headed by another person, and manufacturing is its own division, while research and development is led by scientists. The individuals at the head of these functions are expert in a certain activity and master their art as best they can.

As illustrated in Exhibit 7.2, the Organization-Centric customer model forces the customer to run between expertise bases to get the service they seek.

From a customer perspective, this means that the customer is not subject to the operational excellence of each function. When customers contact the organization with a particular issue, they'd better know in advance exactly what they want. Otherwise, they will subject themselves to the eternal maze—transfer from one part of the organization to the other. "We are responsible for the left nostril, sir. The right ear is another department." This will be the typical response.

Exhibit 7.2 Organization-Centric Customer

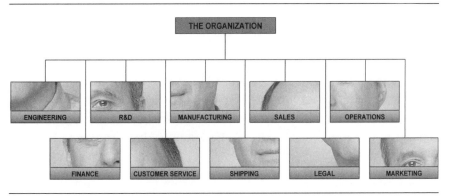

No single function views and manages the customer completely. Sales will do the promising, marketing is in charge of raising expectations, and service will try their best with inadequate resources to fulfill some of the inflated expectations. Accounting will send inaccurate invoices, while shipping will miss deliveries of faulty products designed by R&D and produced by manufacturing. Who is in charge of making sense of all of this? Ask the heads of the different functions, and they point to their operational objectives and how they meet and often beat them. The customers must manage the total value proposition on their own. I am always amazed how often we find organizations with such expertise-based structure; each department brags about their own success while customer satisfaction and repeat business is dropping fast. Somehow, when you look for a person who is responsible for the complete value proposition, you will end up pointing to the customer. We call this phenomenon the *organization-focused customer.* This is the customer who is subject to the organizational structure. His or her job is to fit into the organization chart, making sure there is no deviation from it (while ensuring that he or she adapts to the quarterly reorganizations).

This ridiculous situation is everything *but* customer-centric. No organization can claim to be truly customer focused while such a structure is in place. Jack Welch once said that a hierarchy is an organization with its face to the CEO and its behind to the customer. In reality, in this organization-focused customer phenomenon, the customer is not the center of the organization but a byproduct of it. Employees are reporting to the ever changing organizational chart and not to the customers. This structure rewards internal politics and expertise but not customer focus. Customers are subservient to the company's structure and process. They are components in it. If customers want to take advantage of the company's products or services, they will have to adapt themselves to its structure.

CUSTOMER-FOCUSED ORGANIZATION

For companies that are serious about their customer strategies, it is time to make the leap to Customer-Focused Organizations. These are organizations with a clear alignment around the customer's needs and service objectives. These are organizations that are focused on delivery of great experiences, not on selling them. The changes required to achieve such an organization include:

- *Complete ownership of the value proposition.* An assignment of customer experience management that manages the complete value proposition for the customer from initiation to post-sales, regardless of who delivers each portion of the value proposition. A senior function in the company must take full ownership of managing customer experiences and ensuring their relevance and competitiveness. This function must see the complete picture of the customer and eliminate any silo-based discrepancies in processes and value delivered. It is also this function's responsibility to examine evolving technologies and the competitive landscape to ensure that the experience stays fresh and new and is never commoditized.

- *Complete view of the customer.* One of the byproducts of the silo organization is that individuals in each function have their own view of the customer and fail to see other perspectives. This happens when different databases manage different functions, as opposed to management of the customer across the board. It often leads to stupid situations, such as a salesperson asking for the next order, not knowing that the customer had placed major complaints the previous day. Accounting will issue invoices and often threaten the customer regarding on-time payments, while missing a crucial piece of information: the service department failed to repair the purchased product. An important starting point is to share all the information about a customer across all functions—with *everyone* who touches the customer. Not doing so often leads customers to abuse the system by claiming that the salesperson made certain promises, leaving the company to deliver more than is reasonable and turning the deal into an unprofitable one.

- *Turning the pyramid upside down.* The value to customers today is clearly more on the service side, biased toward personal interactions, rather than focused on the pure service or product delivered. In fact, the products and services themselves are regarded as commoditized, which requires a change in the organizational pyramid. The "infinite wisdom" of the few at the top is no longer sufficient to carry the company through. Companies are heavily dependent on their lowest paid, customer-facing employees to deliver the brand, even as advertising fails to do so. It is time to create a stampede. It is time to unleash the people power in every company. But it requires changing the way we treat, compensate, empower, and educate customer-facing employees.

- *Clear assignment of experiences.* The appropriate part of the customer experience must be assigned to each area of the organization. Although everyone owns the customer, the individuals responsible for each function must understand their portion exactly, as well as its impact on the experience. The impact must be measured often so that everyone can clearly articulate his or her role and responsibility—and be held accountable. Without breaking down the customer experience into specific ownership pieces, the vague statement of "everyone owns the customer" will remain just that: an abstract, meaningless statement.

- *Building the tools.* The organization's tools are often built around a mass-production, functional-expertise structure. A set of tools needs to be put in place that allows a complete view of the customer, with analysis of customer information for better segmentation and customized experiences. The manufacturing process needs to be examined to ensure that it is capable of delivering different services to different customers. From technology for customer segmentation and analysis to customization tools, the organization must ensure that it has the right tools to complement the strategy objectives.

- *Knowing your numbers.* What is the cost of a new customer? What is a customer's annual value? What is the annual cost of servicing customers? What is the cost of a complaint? How much does it cost you to handle an irate customer, including all the escalations and repeat calls? How much do irate customers cost the company in lost business? These are just a few of the many measurements that are crucial to the success of customer strategies. Without the right measurements, such as annual and lifetime value of customers, costs of doing business, maintenance costs, and other key factors, companies will be running blind and will lack the financial foundation to justify the effort. Customer strategies are not about being nice to customers. They are a greedy strategy that takes advantage of loving the customer so much that they have no other choice but to prefer your experiences. A strong financial foundation is required that can justify customer selection and segmentation, as well as the level of service and generosity we *must* afford as part of the relationship. Efficiency-based organizations often fail to find the right numbers, because they measure themselves on total volume and not customer profitability.

- *Building the education process.* Focusing on the customer is everyone's goal, but very few understand what that really means. Employee and manager education is critical for breathing life into this lofty objective. Although skills-based training has been around for a while, very little customer-centric education has been done. What does it really mean? How do we bring it to life every day in the way we operate? How does it affect our decision process? What is the impact on prioritization? These are some of the questions that must be addressed if the organization is seeking to make the leap to a customer-centric business model. Do not assume that your employees understand it on their own, especially if they spent the last few years adhering to an efficiency-based model. They need a double education: one to uproot what they've already learned, including the reasons why it is not appropriate, and then another to introduce the new way of doing business.

In the customer-centric organization illustrated in Exhibit 7.3, all the employees and functions are fully aligned around the customer cause. Individuals in each function see the customer as a whole and also understand exactly their roles and responsibilities in the overall customer experience. In a customer-centric organization there is no delegation of responsibility; everyone is in charge of pleasing the customer. Everything else is secondary to this primary objective.

The customer-centric organization marks a change from employees facing their bosses (each following his own silo-boss, marching to a different tune and rhythm) to *all* employees reporting to a single boss, the customer. The customer can be a wonderfully unifying factor for the organization; petty political games and agendas can be transcended, and everyone can focus on the competitive forces of keeping customers. The power of customer centricity is that it is the one common denominator; none of the organization's

Exhibit 7.3   Customer-Centric Organization

functions can dispute its importance. If planned correctly, the customer-centric model can align everyone in the company to a common goal and a unifying cause.

ASSEMBLER KEEPS THE MONEY

If we examine the differences between the two models described above, we can see clearly how the first, organization-centric model is self-centered and self-serving and how the second truly focuses on the customers. As mentioned before, the rule of thumb is this: whoever assembles the complete value proposition gets the premium. In the organization-centric customer model, the customer is required to collect and assemble the value proposition by running between different departments, trying to get a straight answer to a simple question. This customer perceives the company's value as a commodity and "charges" the company for its lack of full-value ownership, effectively extracting a fee for wasted time and effort by keeping the premium and paying a discounted price for the product or service.

In the second, customer-centric model, the company takes full responsibility to see customers as whole persons and to deliver one unified response to all their experience needs. Thus the company gets to charge a premium price for saving time and effort for the customers and for being able to delight them with wonderful experiences. Customers today no longer choose middle-of-the-road alternatives. The dilution of value proposition as a result of cost cutting efforts forced many customers to take up a defensive efficiency strategy: looking for the cheapest price possible. The savings customers generate from this defensive efficiency strategy are applied by customers elsewhere. These savings are applied to pay a premium price for a great, complete value proposition. Customers simply reallocate their money away from lower value, boring commodities and apply them to those products or services that deliver excellent experiences. So as we discussed, the assembler of the value proposition that delivers the complete experience gets to keep the premium.

To justify a premium price, however, it is not sufficient to have the *inclination* to focus on the customer. An organization-focused customer model will fail, again and again, to achieve the desired premium, because it is geared toward a fractured value proposition waiting to be assembled like a do-it-yourself project by the customer. The way to earn the right to a premium is to make a fundamental change in the organization, one that gives complete ownership of the value proposition to the one who is the boss: the customer.

The choice of assuming full responsibility and making the necessary organizational adjustments is a financial one. It is the difference between selling commodities and allowing the customer to keep the premium, or maximizing the price obtained from customers through maximizing the value. Aligning the organization around the customer is the first step in fulfilling the dream of becoming customer focused. Without organizational change, no strategy will reach the execution stage. It is the organization that breathes life into the promise. If this remains unchanged, the promise will remain unfulfilled.

8

CRITICAL CHOICE 7: DO WE EMPLOY FUNCTIONAL ROBOTS OR PASSIONATE EVANGELISTS?

If I asked you to describe the perfect employee, what would you say? If you are like most employers, you would probably respond with the following wish list:

- Highly motivated
- Team player
- Good communication skills
- Organized
- Self-driven
- Committed
- Competitive
- Thinking out of the box
- Follows instructions
- Hard-working
- Attentive to details
- Deals well with pressure

If your list looks similar to the above, welcome to the land of interchangeable employees. If you check at Monster.com, Hotjobs.com, or any other job search web site, you will discover that your list is no different from the one posted by many other employers. This list would apply to a wide variety of jobs, including (but not limited to) bank tellers, car salespeople, stockbrokers, teachers, firefighters, insurance agents, shipping couriers, customer service representatives, retail associates, and accounting professionals.

Interchangeable employees are versatile. Selection is made on the basis of generic skills, and they can easily work at a wide variety of companies. It is exactly these generic skills that make them interchangeable. On one day they can be working at Toyota and the following day at Wells Fargo bank. In reality, the fact that they can function well in so many places makes them uncommitted to any of them. Their interchangeability qualifies them for many jobs, but at the same time they really qualify for none of them. These employees belong everywhere and nowhere at the same time.

"Qualifies for none?" you ask. Correct. They don't qualify because they lack personal commitment to the job. Their skills can be used to perform in a diversity of jobs, but personal commitment and motivation will be lacking: passion is the missing ingredient. Without the passion, they are merely executing orders and functions. With passion, they are making great companies and creating wonderful lasting relationships.

If your employees are hired on the basis of the criteria listed above and thus fit the interchangeable employee mold, they will probably be able to deliver interactions efficiently, but they will be unable to deliver great experiences. If they do not bring their personal commitment and passion to the work, their execution will lack the most important and differentiating factor, the one factor that creates great experience: passion.

ATTITUDE, NOT SKILL

Most organizations hire on the basis of skills. They believe that skills are crucial to their success, and if they run a non-customer-centric organization, they're right! If, however, customer centricity is at the core of their differentiation and core competence, then skills take a back seat to passion and attitude. When First Direct Bank in the United Kingdom built up the first British phone-based banking system, they decided that their core experience was caring. Thus they did not hire traditional bankers but instead opted for nurses and social workers. These professions included people who had made a personal commitment to caring. I have always found it amazing that certain companies hire on the basis of skills and then expect their training programs to work on people's attitudes. I once asked a client, "If after 18 years at home, their parents failed to change their attitude (with serious motivating incentives such as car keys and grounding—none of which are available to today's employers), what makes you believe that you will succeed in doing so?"

Skills can be easily taught. Attitude and passion are inherent in people. They can be nurtured but not created. You must hire your people on the basis of their personal connection to your cause and core experience. If they love what they do, they will catch up on the skills quickly, and their passion will compensate for many mistakes. If they lack the passion—if they are not personally connected to your world and experiences and find no fulfillment in them—they will fail, despite their skills. The customers will see through them and call their bluff. Customers do not connect to employees who have no passion. The interchangeable employee is a threat to every customer-centric strategy. These employees will do their job efficiently and follow orders, but the customers will not receive great, pleasing experiences. Efficiency is something customers receive from interchangeable employees everywhere. Passionate experiences they crave, but hardly ever receive.

EMPLOYEE EXPERIENCES

It is easy to ask for passionate employees; attracting them, though, is a more difficult task. To reach and attract passionate employees, you need to supply them with a good reason, a reason that will add meaning to their lives and not just utilize them to process interactions. Most companies fail to recognize this critical factor. At the core of the ability to attract passionate people is a compelling employee experience that makes them want to connect and relate.

The employee experience is directly linked to customer experiences. Your employees will not relate to your features or benefits. This is "corporate" stuff, just an irrelevant aspect of corporate greed. They can and will relate to the customer's emotions and aspirations and to the chance you give them to create positive customer experiences. In essence, they will relate to your real business as defined in the customer experience mapping, not to the business you conduct from your features perspective. A strong customer experience and an understanding of the customer mind set and the real impact you deliver is crucial to your ability to present and deliver employee experiences.

Passionate people are attracted to passionate companies that make a difference every day, not to companies that try to fake it with their ads and marketing literature. Companies that hard-code their "making a difference" commitment in their everyday operations will attract and keep the best people.

Often when I discuss this concept with clients, they resist, claiming that their functional jobs are boring and cannot be reinvented into great employee experiences. They see no mission in their jobs and claim that only certain jobs, such as drug research and neurosurgery, have a mission. This argument claims that the vast majority of employees have selected doomed jobs and thus subjected themselves to boredom for the rest of their lives. I beg to differ. Employees did not necessarily make such a choice; they might simply have gotten stuck. Employers, however, have a choice. They can transform the jobs into employee experiences that will maximize the employee's commitment to the company. Every job can be driven by mission rather than function.

Can you imagine a job in which you are asked to draw a cursive L shape all day on a piece of paper? How long would you last? An hour? A day? It sounds like a recipe for insanity. Most people laugh when I present this choice, thinking it is some kind of joke. They cannot imagine doing such a job for more than a few minutes.

Well this is Ayla Wendt's job at Montblanc,[1] the writing instruments company. Ayla has been the nib tester for Montblanc for the last 20 years. Every day she tests the nibs of new fountain pens, ensuring a smooth glide over the paper. The L shape is the curviest letter, so it allows her to examine each nib carefully. If Mrs. Wendt had viewed her job from a nib-testing, functional viewpoint, she would have been bored after a few hours. But she views it through the prism of preparing the pen that will sign the next peace treaty. She is working on the fountain pen that will ink the next merger or acquisition. Mrs. Wendt's pens have played an important role in world events for the last two decades, and she was there to make a difference.

The way Mrs. Wendt is able to connect to the employee experience is through the customer experience. In a world in which pens are almost a commodity (and when you need to write, there are free pens in the conference room or your hotel room), how does a company get away with selling pens for hundreds or thousands of dollars? Montblanc has managed to do it. It has created a powerful customer experience around their writing instruments to differentiate them from the rest of the pack. They understand the growing resistance of customers to the rushed environment in which they are currently operating and living. With technology driving further changes and faster advances, customers often feel lost and disconnected. They feel as if they are no longer in the driver's seat, but in a passenger seat being driven by forces beyond their control. A sense of lost identity is associated with this rushed world.

In days gone by, people believed that if a person touched an object, that object would form a bond with a part of their soul. Today, in an age of progress and mass production, such a thought seems almost absurd.

Absurd that is, until you enter the realm of Montblanc's master craftsmen.[2]

Montblanc positioned itself contrary to this rushed, mass-production trend. Recognizing the hurried mind set of their customers, it promoted the need to take time to reflect. It claims that its tools are an expression of individuality and a way to stop the rushing train of time and technology and just be yourself. For this kind of experience, which is reflected in significantly higher quality and unique designs, customers are willing to pay much more. Ayla Wendt can relate to this level of experience. She wants to help people improve their lives. She wants them to be able to express their individuality, especially in this rushed world. This is why her work makes a difference, and for this cause she is willing to bring her passion to work.

This strong link between employee and customer experiences was well established by our annual Customer Experience Management (CEM)[3] study.

- 80% of the respondents who strongly agreed that their company offers unique services or products agreed that the company deserves the customer's loyalty (versus 0% among those who strongly disagree). This indicates that if they believe in the company's value proposition, they will act accordingly.

- 75% of those who strongly disagreed that their company takes any customer willing to pay agreed that their company deserves the customer's loyalty (versus 44% among those who strongly agree).

- 82% of those who strongly agreed that their company conducts true dialogue with their customers agreed that their company deserves the customer's loyalty (versus 0% who strongly disagreed).

There is a strong correlation between a unique and well-articulated customer strategy and executives' perception of customer loyalty. Many executives still lack a basic understanding of why the customer should buy from their company rather than the competition. This misunderstanding has far-reaching implications for the way employees approach their work and their customers. The greater the clarity about the value and role of the customer, and the more selective the company in their choice of customers, the more executives will be convinced that their company deserves their customers' loyalty. Those who agree that their company deserves their customers' loyalty also deliver loyalty-inducing service and reach new levels of excellence.

The creation of strong employee experiences is directly tied to the quality and uniqueness of the customer experience. The two are not just linked, but rather feed each other. A unique customer experience empowers an employee experience. Employee experiences assist in delivery on the promise to the customer. Understanding this interlinking is critical to developing employee experiences.

EMPLOYEE LOYALTY LEADS TO CUSTOMER LOYALTY

Employee experiences significantly impact on the quality and results of every customer strategy. The inability to design and execute a well-crafted employee experience will damage the organization's ability to differentiate and build a compelling value proposition. These are some highlights from our study:

- 80% of those who agreed that they have the tools and authority to service the customer agreed that their company is committed to customers (versus 37.5% of those who strongly disagreed).

- 75% of those who strongly disagreed that their company accepts any customer willing to pay agreed that their company is truly committed to customers (versus 52% of those who strongly agreed).

- 93% of those who strongly agreed that their executives meet frequently with customers agreed that their company is truly committed to customers (versus 60% of those who strongly disagreed).

- 95% of those who strongly agreed that their role of the customer is well defined agreed that their company is truly committed to customers (versus 45% among those who strongly disagree).

This set of statistics from Strativity Group's annual CEM[4] study supports our previous argument. Employee experiences are linked to customer experiences. The statistics also shed light on a new dimension: for the customer experience to be believable, executive role modeling is required. Despite companies' internal campaigns, employees follow executive actions. They judge by what they see being executed. Top executives' commitment to visit customers is a matter of being a role model and living the mission. There is a strong correlation between these actions and employee perception of an overall commitment to customers. For organizations seeking action and not just slogans, the path to customer experience excellence starts with an amazing employee experience.

EMPLOYMENT HIERARCHY

Employees do not operate on the basis of their skills alone. They have higher, greater needs to fulfill. From self-actualization to a sense of contribution, employees are seeking to make a difference. Employees want to feel as if they are making an impact instead of just processing papers. They want to know that their work is important. To achieve these additional goals, beyond the basic need to put food on the table, employees are seeking a way to connect with a mission and to make a difference.

When we observed employees in a workplace setting, we saw that employees were operating on one of three levels (Exhibit 8.1).

As we see in Exhibit 8.1, each level in the employment hierarchy has distinct characteristics and impacts differently on the business.

1. *Job Seekers.* These are the people at the bottom of the employment hierarchy. They are the people who merely seek a way to pay the bills. They are not committed to the company's success. They are committed to the paycheck. They will do the bare minimum to survive in your company. They will give you the courtesy of drinking the free coffee you serve and taking your paycheck with the minimum effort required. They will also switch jobs as soon as another 5% increase is offered to them. They try to survive the job and they do it on your watch and salary. The job seekers are in high-turnover mode (and if they are not, that is only because they did not find a bigger sucker who will pay them more to do less, and therefore *you* are the *designated* sucker). Because their negative, disposable attitude affects *their* peers and *your* customers, their impact on your business is negative.

2. *Career People.* The career people often confuse us. They make a lot of noise. They seem to be very busy. You want to believe that they contribute and build the business. In reality, they are in selfish mode. They will contribute to the business exactly what they take out of it. They are here to promote themselves and their personal agenda. They

Exhibit 8.1   Employment Hierarchy

	mindset	impact on business	turnover	commitment level
Calling	"my impact on the world"	**STRONG**	very low	higher purpose
Careers	"what is in it for me?"	NEUTRAL	average	selfish
Jobs	"what is my next job?"	**NEGATIVE**	high	survival

are giving you just the right amount to justify what they take back. Their impact on the business is neutral. Don't get confused by the noise; it doesn't equate to results or long-term commitment. They are the ones who will blackmail you for the promotion or threaten to leave for another "much higher paying job."

3. *Calling People.* These employees are on a mission. They are connected to the company's experience, associate and relate to it personally and believe that their work makes a difference. They do what they do not because of the salary or the career, but because it matters. They are changing the world—often just the world of one person, but nevertheless, they view their role through the prism of the difference they make. They are not cynical about their work, they are very proud of it.

For some employees, defaulting to the Career or Job level is simply a matter of lack of a mission. When their employers do not provide such a mission, they default back to skills-based functioning and do the bare minimum to survive. The absence of a strong employee experience and a challenging mission leaves them no choice but to drop to the Career or Job level. For other employees, it is the mismatch between the employee experience delivered by the company and the expected experience that causes them to operate on the basic level and not rise up to the Calling level.

In any case, companies that want to maximize their employees' potential ought to act on both issues: create and communicate powerful missions in their organizations and also weed out the mismatched employees who will distract from the process. In weeding out such employees, they will actually be doing them a favor; hopefully they will find a better, more closely matching employer to fulfill their needs and desired experiences.

We often conduct the following exercise at our seminars: "Let's define the ideal job for you. What would it look like?" The responses usually include:

- Avoiding a commute to the office
- Minimizing e-mail and conference calls
- Working flexible time
- Making a lot of money
- Project-based work rather than ongoing efforts
- No crisis-mode operation
- Limited number of hours at work

At that point, I make the following offer: for $150,000 a year, you get to work from home, no commute, no traffic jams, and no rush hours. You are not required to work a fixed number of hours but can finish the job on your own terms. No e-mails or phone calls are required either. This is your *ideal* job. The job is to clean the sewer in your neighborhood. You cannot hire someone else to do it. This is your job. You finish, you go home. Would you take the job?

Are you still hesitating? Would $200,000 do the trick? How about $500,000? If you accepted the job, how long would you really last? A month? Two months? Six months, tops?

We usually get less than 10% of the participants to take the job regardless of its compliance with the definition of the ideal job. Why is it that people resist the job?

Because they do not work for money only. As per Maslow's needs hierarchy, people operate on multiple levels of need. The physical needs that the salary addresses are only a part of the picture. When the employee meets that basic need, he or she wants other needs to be fulfilled. The problem is that we never design our jobs beyond the level of salary and physical needs. We communicate and address our employees through the narrow prism of salary and leave the rest untouched. Companies never bothered to design and execute a mechanism to address all the employee dimensions. Some companies were actually reluctant to do so, claiming it is not their job. But avoiding a holistic view of the employee is giving up on his or her passion, commitment, and readiness to care. So while we want happy, inspired employees, we are not delivering a reason for them to become that way. We keep it to a basic, salary-driven experience, an experience that is not sufficient to drive employee commitment.

Reengineering the Employee Experience

If you are confident that you have a motivated workforce with a uniquely designed employee experience, just look around you. Are they smiling? There is a simple litmus test that can be applied to provide you with a reality check. You do not need any satisfaction surveys on this matter to validate the word on the street. Just look around you.

Working with clients to define the necessary steps toward customer centricity and customer experience, I have noticed an interesting phenomenon. Top executives were highly receptive to 50% of my message and chose to neglect the other 50%. While appreciating the need to redefine their value proposition and to create fascinating experiences for customers, they were reluctant to do the same for their employees. They wanted to believe that customers need more persuasion and courting because they have more choices, but the same rule does not apply to employees. Employees, executives often believe, will simply follow orders. Therefore, it is unnecessary to spend extra effort to delight them.

An important symptom of this attitude is the lack of tools to conduct the job well. Employees are expected to become automated search machines in their own company's impossible maze of applications and databases. In the process, they waste their own time, as well as their customer's time, and still are not able to focus on delivering excellent, profitable experiences. Executives do not think that providing their employees with modern, fast access is necessary for the employee's experience and satisfaction. As far as management is concerned, employees should be able to do without—without any problems.

The flaw in this thinking is so substantial that I would have preferred that these executives not accept the first 50% of my message and not initiate a customer experience strategy at all. Without employee experiences, there is no customer experience. Employees are the creators of customer experiences. If they do not have great, delightful experiences, they will not deliver the same to customers. Either through product and service innovations or through exceptional customer service, employees are the people who cement the relationships with customers. Employee experiences are the way to make them want to do it. You cannot initiate one without the other—it is that simple.

In reality, employees are not robots. If you order them around, they function only at partial capacity. They will conduct the transactions they were trained (like dogs) to do—but they will not care. Focusing employee efforts on conducting transactions and completing tasks will deplete the company of its best available resource, the passion and willingness to care and help. Your paycheck will go as far as buying their robotic functioning, but it will never reach their hearts. It will never unlock their passion, desire to take risks, willingness to work in teams, ability to excel, or courage to lead change. The key to unlocking their hearts is in their experiences.

By defining the customer experience we are seeking to create and deliver, and by understanding the emotional and aspirational impact these experiences are geared to deliver, organizations can create employee experiences that will attract and retain the quality people who are capable of delivering them.

Reengineering employee experiences requires the same amount of commitment and resources needed to redesign customer experiences. You will increase by more than ten times employee innovation, employee productivity, and (ultimately) customer commitment and loyalty. This initiative will not deliver an incremental impact, but rather an order-of-magnitude result. It is more than worth the effort.

GUIDELINES FOR EMPLOYEE EXPERIENCE REENGINEERING

Nurturing a Culture

As mentioned before, connecting to employees at the lowest level of their needs hierarchy is a common mistake. It leads employees to respond similarly and not care about the rest. Reengineering an employee experience is about unleashing the great power and potential within your people. It is about making them want to give their very best and create amazing customer experiences. Postitive employee experiences are similar to those of customers: making them feel wanted, treating them with generosity, not attempting to create an efficient relationship model, providing interactivity and conversations, and so forth. It is ultimately about nurturing, not management. Remember, people follow your lead. Every day we hear about world leaders, but who ever heard of a world manager?

If management is about forcing the numbers, nurturing a culture is about treating employees in a way that makes them want to do things. Excellence does not come from paying people. In fact, there is not enough money in the world to make an employee smile sincerely. You've seen this face before: the face of a flight attendant forcing herself to smile because they told her to do it. The smile is like a nerve twitch, and the usual result is more contempt than appreciation from the passenger. The passenger senses the insincerity and resents it.

Sincerity only comes from employees wanting to care and make a difference. As a manager, you can facilitate and nurture it through several components that can reinforce your desired culture:

- *An inspiring mission.* Why should employees join your company? What opportunity do you deliver to them to make a difference in the world? What opportunities to do the very best do they get while working for you? These are some of the critical questions a powerful, inspiring mission will address, an inspiring mission that ties in the customer experience and impacts the company is aspiring to deliver.

- *The storybook.* To breathe life into your mission, you need to develop a storybook, one containing stories about the above-and-beyond execution of your employees. The storybook is the road map to your definition of excellence. The more stories you collect, the more frequently the book is updated, and the better your execution. The storybook gives you a way to show your employees that your mission statement is for real and that you insist on bringing it to life; the storybook also lets them visualize and believe in the mission and its desired impact. This is a living book, designed for both further contributions and reading. Managers must incorporate the stories in their staff meetings and frequently reinforce the type of behavior they are seeking.

- *Public recognition.* To encourage such behavior, as per the mission statement, you need to create a mechanism that encourages employees to break the rules, in order to change the way they execute. You need to create a public recognition program that supports your objectives. Your employees need to see that breaking the rules on the customer's behalf is allowed and that rule breaking will be rewarded. One client mentioned that his company had a well-designed program for such activities. When we asked whether it was budgeted, he said it wasn't. The program was in place and was communicated, but it was merely lip service, without much execution power behind it. Another client told us that in the previous three years only two employees had won the award. This is how we have seen many of these programs disappear into a cynical black hole. They become ridiculous, and no one takes them seriously. Like any other idea or vision, this program will be judged on the basis of execution.

- *Leverage their personal preference.* Recently Microsoft and other companies started to permit and even encourage their employees to blog about their work.[5] Employees began to share details about upcoming products and the general atmosphere at the company. These companies realized that they needed better ways to connect with customers. They found that personal, uncensored blogs were a big attraction to customers who were turned off by corporate bureaucracy and were seeking a human touch and a personal warm connection. Allowing employees to connect to customers through their personal preferences enabled the company to leverage both the employees' and the customers' emotions. Such leverage cannot be created or unleashed in other ways. By allowing the blogging, companies are sending a message to customers that they are doing business with humans just like them. To employees, the message is that their preferences and personal life matter and that the company views them as more than their productivity output.

- *Provide a human touch.* Connecting to the employees at their personal level goes a long way toward unleashing commitment. Birthdays, Valentine's Day, and other life events are all opportunities to create a personal bond with employees. If employees see that you bother to care, they will bother to care as well.

Additional infrastructure needs to be put in place to support great employee experiences.

Examine the Tools

Do your employees have the proper and most up-to-date tools to get the job done effectively? During one of our web seminars, we asked participants how many applications their service employees were required to master. To our surprise, more than 35% of the respondents claimed that their customer service employees needed to master more than ten applications. This is an excessively high number. Most executives and CEOs do not work with more than three to five applications, at most. Patch-based information systems that were installed separately, without an overall plan, often provide employees with confusing tools—tools that result in wasted time, tools that hinder their ability to do the job right. It is a simple matter that sends a big message to employees: "You are not important enough for us to invest in better tools for you. Your job is just not that important." When a customer service representative wastes time navigating many old databases to find a simple answer for the customer, he or she realizes that if it was important, the company would have made the appropriate resources available. Taking their cue from the company's lack of investment, employees' level of service and caring becomes aligned with their interpretation of the company's behavior. Employees go by what companies do, not by what they say. They see where resources are invested and assign their priorities accordingly.

If servicing the customer and creating amazing experiences are the top priorities, then it is unacceptable to go to war with antiquated, cumbersome weapons. Equipping employees with such tools is the equivalent of sending an army into a critical battle in 2004 with weapons from 1913. It is a recipe for failure. This is an open invitation for the competition to take over.

Companies continue to seek ways to reduce costs and become more competitive. To do this, they must examine employee experiences to ensure that they have provided them with the necessary tools and access to relevant information, so that the employees become more effective. We often see a patch-oriented approach, whereby companies increase IT system training or even change the compensation plan, just to force employees to master the company's maze of confusing, uncoordinated systems. Stop scratching your right ear with your left hand; it just doesn't make sense. It is time to address the root cause of the problem and automate and modernize these systems, so people can be more effective and productive. Companies can retain their investment in their existing systems and databases, while improving employee and customer experiences significantly. It is time to give the 2004 army the weapons they need to win the battle against the competition, bring the customers home, and keep them there.

There is no better way to start reengineering the employee experience than by showing employees that you are investing in making their work more effective, instead of wasting their time in mundane, unnecessary tasks that can be easily automated.

Empowerment: So Much Is Given, So Little Received

Is that a concept or a mode of operation? Empowerment is one of those odd concepts that every manager claims to deliver, but no employee feels he or she actually receives. Odd, isn't it? Managers claim that they delegate and do not micromanage, but most employees roll their eyes when they hear it, knowing full well that this empowerment never reached their desk. Authority to execute is crucial. If you do not trust your people, do not hire them. If you hire them, do not tie their hands and prevent them from doing their job.

Managers should start viewing empowerment in a new light. The old notion is that the more you empower, the less your job is required. Some managers view empowerment as a way to work themselves out of a job. Nothing could be farther from the truth. Managers need to recognize and accept that empowerment makes them look good. They do not look good because they make all the decisions, but because their employees can do it. The manager's role is to provide guidelines, coaching, and support for their employees' execution.

As a reminder, people empowerment includes:

- Providing authority to resolve problems immediately, without an additional approval process.
- Providing discretionary funds to compensate customers.
- Sharing all information about customers and their business with the organization, to allow full evaluation of the customer's status and needs.
- Supporting employees' decisions in time of controversy.

One of the keys to the success of Bed Bath & Beyond[6] is the focus on the local stores. Each store manager determines about 70% of the products placed on their shelves. The company made a choice to customize their product assortment according to local needs, as opposed to running an economies of scale system that tells the store managers what is good for them. By doing so, the chain truly empowered their managers and held them accountable for performance. The empowerment came with responsibility, as it usually does. But the store managers felt that if they were trusted with such a huge responsibility, they must perform accordingly. Unlike their counterparts in national chains, with the product mix determined by headquarters and thus no real local responsibility for performance, Bed Bath & Beyond managers get to supply what their customers really want, just as they hear it from them every day on the store floor. Empowerment leads to a great experience and a culture of performance and accountability.

Empowerment is one of those management-abused concepts. All managers are convinced they are practicing it. Employees are swearing they've never felt empowered. Companies that seek to create and deliver amazing employee experiences ought to bridge this gap. Examine what empowerment means in your business and start delivering it to your employees.

Ritz Carlton Employee Experience

At the Ritz Carlton Hotels,[7] every employee is empowered to spend up to $2,000 to solve a customer problem. When a guest approaches any one of the ladies and gentlemen (i.e., employees) at any of the Ritz Carlton hotels, that person is empowered to do whatever it takes, up to $2,000, to resolve the problem immediately. The hotel employee is not expected to delegate the problem to the proper department or to ask permission from his or her manager, but rather to do whatever it takes to get the problem resolved. He or she owns the problem until it is solved.

With this policy, the Ritz Carlton Hotels demonstrate their trust in their people. Employees are carefully selected for their ability to apply the common-sense judgment required to solve problems. The Ritz Carlton Hotels also signal to their people that there is no excuse not to satisfy guests, and no procedure or manager should prevent them from achieving a positive total customer experience.

It is better to err on the side of generosity and make sure employees have more, rather than less. There is a great likelihood that for every *one* mistake they make by overstepping their authority, they will also please and surprise 100 customers, who will be amazed by your employee's ability to solve problems quickly and satisfactorily.

Remember: If you do not trust your people, do not hire them. If you hired them, give them the tools to excel. After all, their success is your success.

TRAINING IS FOR DOGS— EDUCATION IS FOR PEOPLE

Education—much has been written about the training of sales and customer services professionals. Yet each time we work with a client, we find the same symptoms appearing repeatedly.

The training program represents a set of restrictions that tie the hands of the employees and provide the best excuse why *not* to service customers well. Built with control in mind, the training programs are about following procedures and adhering to guidelines. Thus the employees are receiving a message that the procedures are what matter. Rarely do we see principles-based education that allows employees to use common sense to solve customer problems and deliver a pleasing experience.

When you train your people with procedures and rules, you train them to focus on adherence to corporate matters. In the process, you strip them of any form of responsibility, as they realize that the only responsibility they have is to follow the rules. Usually, performance evaluations reinforce this priority over any other.

So let's start with the basics: terminology. *Training* is for dogs. We train dogs to repeat actions and not to be creative. *Education* and *learning* are for people. We educate them to assume responsibility and contribute to the company, and then we must allow them to do so. Let's change the terms.

When joining 1-800 Flowers, new call center agents are handed a thick book full of thank-you letters. As they read them, they are told that their job is to accumulate more thank-you letters. How they do it is up to them. Ultimately, 1-800 Flowers defines its business from the perspective of pleasing customers and thus instructs its agents to conduct themselves as thank-you letter generators. The other interesting aspect to the educational experience at 1-800 Flowers is the fact that they do not use procedures, but rather examples and stories to instruct. The stories allow new agents to relate to the required work and desired experiences and enable the agents to repeat them easily during their interactions with customers.

A good employee education program should focus on providing financial data that empower employees to execute well and then allow them to use their common sense to resolve customer issues. The most important information your employees must have includes:

- Company financial data
- Product or service profit margins and costs
- Customer history
- Customer profitability
- Customer preferences
- The average cost of a complaint

Without this information, employees cannot distinguish between customers. They cannot deliver different services to different customers. They are operating without a commercial, business context. Thus they are bound to deliver mediocre service and experiences because they cannot justify doing a better job. The financial measures listed above will allow employees to use their judgment and apply it to their decisions and solutions. By having this information readily available, they are able to solve customer problems faster and more effectively and deliver service in proportion to the customer's value.

Employees who are empowered with the right financial information are enjoying a better employee experience: they know that their employer trusts their commercial judgment. It is a symbol of their participation in the overall business responsibility.

To complement the commercial information, successful customer-centric learning programs focus on several other aspects to ensure employee readiness. These aspects include:

- *Skills.* After passion and excitement have been established, the employee needs to acquire the skills to work effectively. Skills should be taught and mastered now, and not before.

- *Caring: Using examples and success stories.* Caring is difficult to teach. But through stories and examples, employees can visualize what the company is seeking. Through real-life examples, companies can and should bring to life their intentions regarding employee caring.

- *Role playing.* Since every customer interaction has multiple dimensions, and one is never the same as another, role playing is important to build employees' confidence that they are capable of dealing with the situation. Role playing will also provide insights into the customer's mind set and concerns.

- *Commercial knowledge.* In addition to the financial factors mentioned above, any additional financial knowledge can improve employees' overall understanding of the state of the business. Their ability to utilize the knowledge to deliver the right experience to each customer will also be sharpened.

- *Dealing with exceptions.* Exceptions are part of human life. Each customer is a unique person, equal to no other. Customers often do not fit the mold created by the corporation. Dealing with them requires a dedicated education with examples and guidelines.

- *Coaching.* After the initial education session, coaching will be required. The coaching should reinforce existing principles, remind employees how to utilize the financial knowledge to distinguish between customers, and guide employees in correcting mistakes. Reinforcement of good behavior to instill confidence in new employees is another coaching dimension.

- *Creating a culture of excellence.* The overall education program should be supported by the concept of excellence, using tools and reminders about the company's excellence goals. Stories of excellence should be collected and distributed. These stories, gathered from the employees' own behavior, can reinforce the organization's commitment and ability to deliver on its promised experience. They should encourage all employees to continue the pursuit of excellence and raise the overall excellence standards.

Understanding Principles versus Procedures

Whereas most common learning programs focus on procedures and rules, they must shift to providing employees with guiding principles and then allow employees to do the right thing in every unique scenario. As this table indicates, this is not just about semantics. There are fundamental differences between a procedures-based training system and a principles-based learning program.

Principles	Procedures
Provide guidelines	Highly controlled mechanism
Allow resolving out-of-box problems	Address predefined problems
Empower employees	No employee ownership
Deliver faster resolution	Minimal trust required
Flat resolution system	No common sense required
Require high level of trust	Evaluate employees on adherence
Require common sense	to the rules
Create greater employee responsibility	Delay resolutions owing to
Evaluate employees on breaking	escalation
the rules	Multi-tier resolution system

Training is about controlling employees and holding them responsible for executing procedures. Education is about teaching them the business ground rules and then allowing them to use their common sense to delight customers. These are two different ways of dealing with your employees. The former sends a message that their primary focus is to follow the rules; the latter bestows upon them full responsibility to care and to solve customer problems.

Review your training program and weed out the unnecessary rules and regulations. Replace them by teaching commercial guidelines, so that your people understand your business and financial considerations and apply them as they service customers. They need to understand that different customers are treated differently, based on their total business with the company. They should understand your margins and annual customer value so they can select the right compensation level for certain problems. Instead of controlling them, free them to execute through better understanding of the business principles.

I recall a recent trip with Virgin Atlantic from New York to London in which the entertainment system did not function. To my amazement, we were immediately offered free duty-free or 10,000 miles in compensation, which was at different levels for economy- and business-class passengers. The flight purser told me that there was no procedure for such incidents. However, the cost of opening a complaint was 25 pounds sterling (approximately $40), and that was *before* the cost of resolution. The flight attendants applied their common sense and decided to solve the problem faster—even before the customers complained. (What a concept!)

If it is so simple, why are companies not doing it? One reason is obvious: they do not have all the data. Most companies have never calculated the cost of a complaint. But that is the easy part. The hard part is the delegation of power. Managers often feel that if they empower employees with this information, they will relinquish too much power and become irrelevant. It is time for such managers to understand that power is not a zero-sum game. The more you give, the more you have. The better your employees perform and delight customers, the better the executives will look. It is time to put the responsibility back where it belongs—in the hands of the people who deliver the service. Empower them with the knowledge required and set them free to execute.

DELIGHT THEM: THEY ARE HUMAN TOO

Are you taking advantage of the complete employee? Are you tapping into their passion and willingness to assist and care, or are you just tapping into their ability to conduct functions like a robot? To unleash the best in your people, you must treat them like customers. You must give them the same surprisingly amazing treatment that makes them want to excel and give you the best they have to give. You may force employees to conduct transactions, but you cannot force them to smile sincerely. The sincere smile that builds a great customer experience comes from their personal reservoirs. You cannot force it, but you can nurture it.

Treat them well, surprise them with your care, and they will care for your business. Show them your commitment, and they will reciprocate.

COMPENSATION: FOLLOW THE MONEY TRAIL

As you reengineer the employee experience, what are the criteria upon which you determine compensation and incentives? For some companies it is straight base pay. This approach reinforces indifference to employees and signals that extra effort is useless. Assuming that employees will go above and beyond for the standard salary, without any incentives, is wishful thinking.

Another prevailing approach reinforces the productivity and efficiency model. This model provides compensation on the basis of quantity and not quality. This quantity will come in the form of achieving sales quotas, production quantities, service cases closed, or number of leads. However you look at these compensation plans, you will clearly get the message that the production floor is in action. Usually little or no emphasis is placed on quality and customer acceptance. These companies will never achieve meaningful customer focus, because their compensation plan is in direct conflict with customer centricity goals. Ultimately, employees will do what they are paid to do, and little else.

The performance evaluation and the compensation plan must reflect the customer centricity objectives to ensure the strategy's success. In Chapter 10, Critical Choice 9, the guidelines for a customer-centric performance evaluation and compensation program, are explored.

As you approach the process of reengineering your employee experiences, be aware of the fact that it is highly likely that your employees will be suspicious, skeptical, cynical, or all of the above. They deserve to be. After being told during the 1990s that they were the critical asset of the company, they saw a different face of the company in the early 2000s. An unfeeling, faceless machine gave them the cold shoulder as it focused on cost reduction and treated them as another source of cost. It takes time to rebuild trust. You will need to demonstrate with investment, and not T-shirts or posters, that you are launching a program that will last. But if your efforts are sincere, your employees will eventually believe you and buy into it.

Employees share an important attribute with customers: they are human. This attribute allows them to connect with customers like no web-based self-service system or IVR ever will. Employees can create memorable, positive, emotional experiences in customers that win them over and beat the competition. To achieve those objectives, you must address two critical factors: providing the tools and unleashing the passion. By providing your employees with modern efficient tools, you send them a signal regarding the importance you place on their work and role. This new experience will be a major step toward unleashing their passion and commitment as well.

If your company is building a case for a customer experience strategy and you are counting on the great financial rewards that it can deliver by reduction of customer churn and increase in monthly business per existing customer, do not forget the critical factor. The employee's experience is the path to customer experiences. One cannot happen without the other. Do not fall into the old shortcut trap. Providing great employee experiences is a wonderful way to demonstrate to your employees the type of customer experiences you are seeking to deliver. They will reciprocate all your efforts in the form of enhanced customer experience. Create a great experience for your people, and they will take care of the rest.

Endnotes

1. "The Soulmakers" (Montblanc).
2. Ibid.
3. CEM Annual Global Study by Strativity Group.
4. Ibid.
5. *www.microsoft.com.*
6. Nanette Byrnes, "What's Beyond for Bed Bath & Beyond?" (Union, NJ: *BusinessWeek,* January 19, 2004), p. 46.
7. Duff McDonald, "Roll Out the Blue Carpet" (New York: *Business 2.0,* May 2004), p. 53.

9

CRITICAL CHOICE 8: POST-SALES DIALOGUE AND SERVICE — DO WE REALLY CARE?

Lip service disguises the harsh truth of Critical Choice 8, as it does for other choices. Despite all the commitments made in pre-sales conversations, most companies are not staffed to live up to those commitments. How often have you seen the company's president lavishly commit to sales prospects, while your peers were rolling their eyes in disbelief? If this scenario sounds familiar, your company is one of those organizations in which post-sales activities are merely a way to extract money from customers, a necessary evil the company has not found a way to avoid.

The whole post-sales organization is traditionally understaffed, because the CFO perceives it as necessary overhead required to collect on accounts receivable. Companies are never ready to live up to the promises, let alone to build true, long-term dialogue with the customers. They are, in fact, the masters of fire-fighting and closing cases. They are the ones left with the check when the deal is closed and celebrated.

It is exactly because so many companies are not staffed and organized for post-sales excellence that it is a huge opportunity. Creating a true dialogue that will be a building block for a long-term relationship is an open issue, inviting companies to differentiate themselves not on the smoothness of their sales force but on the execution of their service people.

This critical choice begs attention, and not just because of the broken delivery system at most companies. It is critical because during the sales process, we heighten expectations. We are causing our customers to believe we have a sincere interest in true partnership with them, knowing quite well we don't have the ability (behind the great façade) to deliver on those promises. You are better off without the promises, because at least your customers will not be disappointed.

Organizations must face this critical choice and decide where they stand. Developing expectations, only to later disappoint customers, is not a way to run a business.

CULTURE OF THE NEW

The failure to deliver past the signature on the purchase order is not new. It stems from several problems, among them the *Culture of the New*. As individuals and organizations, we love new things. We love to launch a new program, we admire our rainmakers who bring new customers, and we always look for the new product or idea. New is culturally admirable and desirable. The more new we have, the better we do.

Maintenance, however, is a different story. Maintenance is about old things. It is about boring, repetitive stuff. It is not as exciting as the new. It is not as appealing as the new. No one was ever promoted for keeping the old. We do not reward maintenance as we reward the new—new sales, new product launches, new branches, new global expansion. New is what we love to do. Maintenance is what we must do (and often do against our will).

It is exactly this culture—a culture that spans both our private and professional lives—that causes us to overlook and underestimate the post-sales function and its importance. "These are old-news customers. We are focusing on the new customers." Like a typical silo-based organization, we throw the responsibility for the recently new, currently old customers over the fence for the maintenance people to deal with (hopefully with minimal expense).

TAKING CUSTOMERS FOR GRANTED

The concept of customer relationships is plagued with another problem that impacts on post-sales service. At a corporate level, we talk about customers in terms we would absolutely refuse to accept if they were applied to us. *Customer acquisition* is one example. No customer wants to be acquired. No customer would agree to be in a relationship in which he or she is regarded as acquired. Would you?

When we use such terms, we move beyond semantics into action—the way we treat customers. The moment a customer is acquired, we move to the next "target." We take the acquired customer for granted and stop nurturing for the next level. Why should we, if the acquisition process is complete? Customers, however, represent a journey, not a destination. They must be treated as long-term investments and not quarterly results fillers.

Although you are probably not admitting to these truths and sticking to your slogan, "the customer is a lifetime commitment," a simple litmus test will prove this point. Check your sales compensation plan and the sales resources allocations. Is it true that new customers command higher rewards? What about the people allocated to service for existing customers versus those focusing on new customers? Isn't it usually the case that new customers are assigned to the better rainmakers, while new salespeople are acting as account executives, "saddled" with maintaining existing accounts? If this is the case, your slogans and high-level intentions did not pass the test. The slogans are good for the wall, but they don't constitute an executable plan you can run your business by.

The moment we understand this truth, the investment in post-sales service and dialogue will make sense. In fact, the investment will no longer be regarded as post-sales. Post-sales service will become an enabler for the next sale and thus will justify the resources required. Such resources will no longer be costs against the initial sale but additional business to be generated more cost-effectively through better delivery of quality service and products. This is a different way of looking at the total customer value and what is necessary to deliver it. The sale is merely a starting point, not the endgame. The real business and total lifetime value will be determined by the service.

FOUR CHECKPOINTS FOR DELIVERING TRUE EXPERIENCES AND RELATIONSHIPS

From a customer perspective, there are several checkpoints or milestones that will testify to the sincerity and long-term prospects of the relationship. Today's customers are suspicious of the courting signs and early excitement. They have been there many times, with a sweet-talking salesperson confirming that everything will be all right, only to disappear one second after the order is signed and paid for. Customers have developed a numb spot for the exaggerated promises arriving through advertising and other marketing and sales vehicles. Before committing to a relationship, customers now demand to see true commitment on the part of the vendors. Because of a long history of high expectations and crushing results, they now apply more demanding criteria to ensure they are not being fooled again.

The four checkpoints (see Exhibit 9.1) customers apply are:

1. Complaint Resolution
2. Insight Management

Exhibit 9.1   Customer Dialogue: The Four Checkpoints

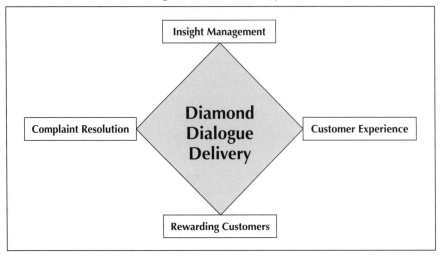

3. Rewarding Customers

4. Customer Experience Index

If vendors pass these checkpoints, they will win the customers' hearts and be able to establish a profitable, long-lasting relationship. Failing them will prove to the customer once again that vendors are never sincere and should not be trusted. If you are faced with a customer who has a long history of disappointment, you should not be discouraged. In fact, this situation represents a big window of opportunity. It is exactly because many companies fail in these crucial tests that you should view it as a key way to differentiate and build loyalty. When your competition increases its marketing budget, you should counter by increasing your post-sales budget. Win the most important battles, the ones that can prove your sincerity and commitment. No ad campaign can establish your commitment level like great service, delivered consistently, that addresses the four key checkpoints.

Let's examine each to gain a better understanding of the customer's expectations and how to address them.

Complaint Resolution

Complaints are often misunderstood by many organizations. Complaining customers are often perceived and treated as a bunch of whiners seeking some freebies. From the CFO perspective, these are bad customers seeking to reduce margins. Often regarded as annoying and distracting, complaints and complainers are handled accordingly. Organizations fail to recognize the real issues and make it very difficult for these "freebie seekers" to get their wishes.

In reality, complaints represent something completely different. Are there some freebie seekers out there? Sure, as in any system, there will be abusers. But do they represent the majority? I would argue that they do not—and the majority should not be penalized for the few abusers. Complaint perceptions in companies must change. When we understand that only 2% of upset customers actually bother to complain, we can understand that complaints represent a last vote of confidence in the company. They carry the message: "We still believe in you and our relationship. We are giving you a last chance to fix it." Unlike a larger group of customers, which just gives up and does not bother giving you a second chance, complainers are people who still believe in you. They are usually customers with a greater stake and vested interest in the relationship (a more profitable, longer relationship) who are seeking a reason not to switch to the competition. They are calling you with a complaint, asking you to provide them with a reason to stay loyal.

If we subscribe to Philip Kotler's claim that a new customer is five times more expensive than an existing one, then what are we doing to stratify those few who are giving us a second chance? How are we structured to pass the first critical test to prove our true commitment to the customer?

Because of the negative perception of complainers as freebie seekers, complaints are handled in an inconsistent and suspicious way by many organizations. Examine your own company's guidelines. You will probably find an annoying, trust-busting process that ties the hands of your employees, preventing quick resolution.

When reviewing complaints, we identified two types: solvable and unsolvable. The solvable complaints are easy. A customer calls and complains about an inaccurate bill. You should solve this request quickly on the first call, either by explaining the reason for the inaccuracy or by adjusting the bill to reflect the accurate situation. This should be done with full empowerment to the employee to apologize and potentially provide a small compensation as an apology for the mistake. Make sure that your employees have the power to solve such complaints right away. Flatten the escalation process and shift power and education to the front-line employees who take the first call.

Unsolvable complaints, however, represent a puzzling question. Why are people calling to submit their unsolvable complaints? Is it to let off steam? I would argue that they have done so already with their friends and family (as such, they spread bad reputation and increase the cost of new customers), who already patted their bruised egos and showered them with sincere pity. Why would these customers subject themselves to unnecessary hold time with lousy music and annoying messages, only to be talking to a faceless, uncaring employee?

The reason is that they are trying to rebalance their situation. As long as they live with the consequences of your mistakes, their lives are not balanced. They feel as if they are carrying on their shoulders a burden that you should own. They are living with your responsibilities. They do not like it. They want to reach an equilibrium in which each side lives with the consequences of its deeds. They are asking you to assume responsibility. Offering a fake "sorry" will not cut it, or even a sincere "sorry." It will actually reinforce their feeling of imbalance and living with the consequences of something they did not do or should not be responsible for.

The answer is this: they are looking for action, not words. The first action they are seeking is some form of a monetary or valuable compensation that represents a physical assumption of responsibility. It can be as simple as a music CD or a magazine subscription, but it has to be something you deliver to them to represent your assumption of the responsibility. This physical exchange is what helps them rebalance their feelings and see that you are a responsible participant in the relationship, because you are willing to take charge of your actions. The compensation should, of course, be proportionate to the price paid and the severity of the mistake. We are not advocating a losing proposition in which a $25 item should be compensated for with a $500 gift. The customer is not expecting that. But five recalls of a $45,000 car should not go unnoticed or compensated for with a $3 coupon for coffee, either.

The other expected action is fixing the situation for future customers. Complaining customers are taking valuable time from their busy schedule to communicate with you because this is their contribution to the relationship. They want to see it growing and improving, not deteriorating. Their complaints are requests for attention to the issue and assurance that it will be fixed. Awareness is not sufficient. Customers want you to remedy the situation. They are willing to live with a one-time mistake and grant you the courtesy of forgiveness (of course, you helped them rebalance their situation), but they will not be willing to live through the same mistake again. Even a money-back guarantee will not be sufficient to get them back. Often, customers do not even bother with the money-back guarantee. They simply take their business elsewhere. Companies must internalize the complaints and work to avoid them in the future. Notifying the customer of any action taken with regard to their complaints will go a long way to ensure their loyalty and prove to them how serious you are. It will help you pass the first checkpoint.

Customer Insight Management

How often have you visited a hotel and noticed a familiar brochure? The title reads something like "Only 60 Seconds of Your Time" or "Your Opinion Matters," or "We Truly Want to Know." Sound familiar? These are the customer feedback cards. How often did you bother to fill them out? Probably never. Why did you so rudely ignore these pleas for a piece of your mind? Because you thought it was a waste of time. Because deep down, you knew they don't really care and no one will pay attention. You might as well put it straight in the paper shredder.

The problem with customer feedback is that companies are not structured to deal with it. Unless it is a great compliment, they have no process or workflow to do something with the ideas/complaints/insights provided by customers. If a customer calls your contact center right now with a great idea, what would the receiving employee do with it? Where would a customer e-mail containing an insight be forwarded to? What is really happening to the thousands of customer comments you receive every month?

This is almost a rhetorical question; I would not want to embarrass you. But this is exactly the reason why customers are skeptical about your claims of wanting a true partnership. If you seek a true dialogue, then do not stop short of action. Do something with it. Take the comments, evaluate them, and implement them if they make business sense. If there is a partnership, then customer opinions should dictate the company's agenda. To do so, companies must establish a workflow that channels customer insight to the right people and assigns them the role of evaluation and implementation. This workflow should prioritize the different insights and address those that make business sense. Companies may choose to establish a virtual focus group of customers to help them assess the importance of each insight and prioritize the issues the company should focus on to ensure maximum impact. By bringing multiple ideas into the focus group, they will establish an element of interactivity that demonstrates to customers their concern about the relationship and its destiny.

After assessment and implementation, customers should be told what has happened with their insights. Even if the insight was rejected, customers should be informed that it was taken seriously. The creation of an idea-management system does not mean that the company gives free license for every customer to demand the outrageous. All evaluations and decisions must be made in the context of profitability and pleasing customers. Adding a democratic ranking process can assist in isolating the few noisy customers and focusing on the maximum impact to the majority to ensure that the company is not losing focus because of a few real whiners. If you want to prove to customers that you are serious about long-term relationships, start taking their insights seriously.

For example, why shouldn't you add a new section to your web site and annual report that will read "So far this year, we have evaluated 56,900 customer ideas and implemented 12,587 ideas, which resulted in more than $45,000,000 in savings and product improvements"? This statement will go a long way to get you past the second checkpoint.

Rewarding Customers

If you have defined the customer role, you know by now the optimal length of a customer relationship and the annual or lifetime value of a customer. Let's say that last year, several customers surpassed those expectations. They reached a ten-year milestone, while your expectations were only five years. Other customers have doubled their business with you, while you only expected a modest 10% increase in business. What have you done for these customers? How did you reinforce their behavior and demonstrate to them that you do not take this behavior for granted?

I am not referring to the token, generic chocolates you ask your secretary to send every year, or the free calendar you produce, which serves more as a free advertisement for your company than as a token of appreciation. I am referring to serious, considerate gifts that show thought and appreciation.

We somehow forget to demonstrate our appreciation for what they did for us all year long. But this is not the odd part. The odd part is the fact that, come next year, we will expect them to do the same and even more.

Why is it that companies forget such an important customer checkpoint? There are several reasons for this puzzling behavior:

- *Lack of Knowledge.* We simply do not know who doubled their business with us this year and who left us for the competition. I am not referring to the anecdotal story of one big order, but to a systematic mechanism that shows us customer performance and compares it with the previous year's performance. Between lack of tools and lack of discipline, we simply do not know.

- *Customer as a Destination and Not as a Journey.* As much as we hate to admit it, we never structured the customer relationship to include long-term planning and measurements. We rush from order to order and always assume there will not be another one. Every customer order is regarded as the achievement of a superstar salesperson and not as a building block in a relationship. Thus we never bother to look at the long-term view but instead reward the occasional order and not the accumulation of the relationship.

- *Customer Is Taken for Granted.* This we will never admit, but our culture glorifies new customer acquisition. When our sales culture is all about new customers, and current customers are sent to low-level account managers, the message is obvious. Our sales force places emphasis on new accounts and forgets the existing ones. It is called taking the customer for granted.

Rewarding customers is about maintaining and nurturing the relationship. It is about sending a message of sincere appreciation. It is about making a greater bond for the future. But most of all it is a financial move to retain your most profitable customers and keep the revenues flowing. Think about rewarding customers as a competitive weapon. How much discount would you provide to beat your competition? Now you have the opportunity to beat the competition *before* they show up.

Rewarding customers should address the behavior you are seeking to reinforce and repeat. You must design a set of criteria that you will use to reward customer behavior. Examples of such criteria may include:

- *Self-Reliance and Self-Service.* If your customer is now more self-reliant and consumes fewer resources make sure you thank him or her. You must demonstrate your appreciation for the efforts the customer made to comply with your request. Otherwise the message you send is: "I want you to do most of the work, but I will still charge you the same"—not exactly an enticing message to keep the relationship going.

- *Relationship Longevity.* If your average customer stays with you for three years and a small group of customers stays for five years, it is a reason for reward and celebration. You want them to stay longer, and they want to know you do not forget them as you pursue new customers. Find a way to share your appreciation with them. It will pay off.

- *Increase in Business.* If customers have doubled their business with you this year, they need to know you took notice of their actions. They need to know that you value their efforts. After all, such customers are few.

- *Meaningful Insight.* Customers often deliver important ideas that then turn into new features or products. Don't forget to say thank you. There is no reason you should benefit from the idea and leave the customer out. What message would that send to other customers with ideas?

- *Referrals and Recommendations.* For those customers who helped you generate more business from their friends and family, it is time to say thank you as well. When you consider the savings associated with the lower cost of gaining a new customer, rewarding customers seems like a great bargain. If you want more referrals, reinforce the behavior by showing your true feelings.

At Money Mailers Corporation, there is a concierge service dedicated to rewarding customers. These rewards include:

- A congratulatory letter signed by the president, with a gift basket, upon each five-year anniversary.

- Another letter to recognize performance milestones and achievements. The more they succeed, the more they are personally recognized.

- Celebration of birthdays with a card and phone call from an executive.

- Recognition of wedding anniversaries by a gift basket and an executive staff letter.

Money Mailers does not take anything for granted nor leave anything to chance. They are recognizing both the personal and professional milestones of their customers and making sure customers realize their business is precious and important to Money Mailers.

Rewarding customers is not about being nice. It is about being greedy. It is a way to reinforce customer commitment to you through a demonstration of appreciation. It is the most affordable weapon you can deploy to get customers to continue and even increase the behavior you value the most; it is a way to retain those who have delivered amazing performances deserving of appreciation. First you have to find out who they are, and then add them to your shopping list. Rewarding customers is about demonstrating to them that you notice their investment and commitment to the relationship.

Customer Experience Index

Customer satisfaction surveys are a great way for managers to get their bonuses. Often, when presented with a customer survey, we ask whose compensation is tied to the results. The questions and possible answers are usually crafted to support certain results. That is why we often regard them as

Compensation Support Surveys. However, the Customer Experience (CE) Index is a living, frequently updated voice of the customer that impacts on execution. It is a mechanism built around multiple sources (such as customer surveys, quality monitoring, and live interviews) that create a live view of the company status. Each department is charted against their piece of the experience and assigned to improve it. The departments then receive results based on their piece of the experience. The index will cover a wide variety of issues, including:

- Product design
- Manufacturing quality
- Delivery issues
- Accounting issues
- Sales issues
- Competitive issues
- Operational issues
- Agent's service capabilities
- Channel/distribution issues

The index will also include Customer Action-Based Factors to support commitment. As many studies demonstrate, satisfaction is not an indicator of future purchases. That is why we move to customer action measures to ensure, through customer actions, that they are indeed committed to the relationship and not just replying about a temporary perception that is subject to change.

To establish a successful CE Index, consider the following guidelines:

- Make clear to every employee where they fit in the measurement system.
- Clarify your targets to employees.
- Clarify your goals to customers to ensure participation.
- Provide frequent, visible results.
- Make results easy to understand and view.
- Provide personalized results, if possible.

As indicated in Exhibit 9.2, the design of the CE Index should strike a balance between the organizational factors measured in the index and the departmental factors. Organizational factors are not sufficient, as they will be too far removed from everyday departmental execution. When you are focusing on such factors alone, departments may disregard them or fail to

Exhibit 9.2   Organization Experience Index

see their specific responsibility. Accounting may view customer satisfaction as a sales/customer service responsibility only. Each part of the organization must know exactly what part of the customer experience they own and are responsible for. The measurements of each function should be reflected in the factors that represent that ownership of their piece of the total customer experience. Complemented by organization-wide factors, each department can align its efforts and everyday activities with the complete customer experience. Departments will also have the incentive to see and cooperate around the bigger picture of the company represented by customer action measurements such as growth in wallet share.

These customer action factors will include:

- Increase in customer overall wallet share
- Decrease in customer complaints
- Increase in customer acceptance
- Increase in customer referrals
- Increase in customer interactions with the organization
- Overall growth in business per customer
- Change in cost of new customer acquisition

- Change in customer attitude toward the brand/organization
- Increase in customer thank-you letters
- Increase in customer ideas and insights
- Increase in customer upgrades
- Increase in sales of accessories
- Increase in cross-selling results

All these factors indicate that customers are voting with their actions to demonstrate satisfaction and appreciation. This is no longer about passing judgment on company functions, as many customer satisfaction surveys require; it is about measuring the contribution of each part of the company to the experience and total value of the relationship, as reflected in customer actions and not perception. It is a healthier way to assess your future business and success.

REQUIRED TOOLS

It is only after a well-devised strategy and operational plan are put in place that the question of the required technology tools should arise. There is no doubt that technology tools such as Customer Relationship Management (CRM) and quality monitoring can demonstrate impressive improvements in the overall way in which the company and its employees deliver customer value. From savings of time to expansion of reach, these tools can improve customer convenience and satisfaction.

To deliver a successful customer-centric strategy, companies will need to ensure they have the right technology tools for the strategy. These tools are the ones that will empower employees (at every touch point) to understand their pool of customers, segment them properly, and to customize information and solutions. The tools are also used for giving employees the right knowledge at the right time to treat customers in a more personal way. It is with these tools that employees will be able to deliver different services to different customers. These technologies can quickly provide employees with the information they need to cross-sell new products to existing customers, maximizing their value in the process.

Some of these tools might already exist within your organization, but probably not with the full feature set to conduct the knowledge development you need. In other cases, the tools are not fully exploited to deliver the maximum value to your organization and your customers. Either way, you ought to reexamine the available tools and their utilization and then identify what is missing. Your consideration of technology tools for customer-centric strategies should include:

- *Updated Customer Database—Know Your Customers.* Make sure that your database is flexible and allows you to add more qualitative information about your customers. Databases and CRM tools provide this type of functionality. They also allow you to provide a unified, complete picture of the customer across different touch points and drive better knowledge among employees as they serve the customers.

- *Integration Tools.* Integrate customer information to create a unified view of the customer. Companies often run separate databases and applications for different functions. These separate sources of information cause confusion and mistakes. They always lengthen service time. Integration tools allow you to create a unified view of the customer across different departments and therefore a higher level of accuracy and speedy service.

- *Business Analytics Tools Such as Customer Segmentation and Real-Time Alerts.* These tools will allow you to segment your customer base better, understand and track patterns of behavior, and alert your employees to special customers and segments. Geographical differences, purchasing patterns, genders, and hobbies are some of the segmentation possibilities you should have available to help you understand and service your customers better. They will also provide you with the capability to flag platinum and gold customers; then every employee knows they should be treated differently, at a different level of problem resolution. Without that knowledge, the service delivery becomes uniform and the customer becomes a number, not a human with history and behavior patterns. These tools should also allow you to target offers more personally to customers and enhance your chances of repeat business and cross-selling.

- *Monitoring and Evaluation Tools.* Keep track of employee performance. These tools allow you to capture interactions as they happen and provide visual and story-like coaching by providing better guidance through examples. Employees should be allowed to evaluate themselves with these tools, which will allow companies to see a more complete picture of the gap between companies' and employees' perceptions of service. The monitoring tools will also allow you to create a repository of great interactions for future employee education. In addition, such tools will reduce the cost of new employee confusion and mistakes.

- *Customer and Employee Surveys.* Measure your performance from the customer and employee perspectives regularly. This should not be an annual event, but an ongoing, just-in-time activity that tracks changes and gaps to drive faster execution.

- *Coaching and Self-Learning Tools.* Empower your people to learn and bridge their gaps. These tools have the potential for allowing employees to reeducate themselves without the embarrassment of asking for help. They can do so at their own pace with no impact on performance. Since they replace classroom training, the self-learning tools are cost-effective and flexible.

- *Financial Data.* Provide knowledge to your people. To deliver experiences that are both pleasing and profitable, your employees need to know important financial factors, such as the cost of complaints and product margins. Often these measurements do not exist. To empower your people to serve and delight, you will need to get the tools to help you identify the costs and make this knowledge available to your people.

- *Process Assessments.* Reduce customer hassles through process simplifications. Audit your self-service and automated call systems to ensure that customers are not hassled.

COMPLETE RELATIONSHIP ACCOUNT

When a customer provides you with a referral, what do you do with it? At best, you follow up on the referral and close business. Where is it recorded for future reference? When a new customer insight was implemented, where is that fact recorded for future reference? We ought to keep a record of all activities in the collective memory of the company in order to see the customer in a holistic way.

The vast majority of customer databases are transaction based. They view the customer through the narrow prism of purchase history but fail to provide a complete, holistic view. Thus we miss business opportunities and often upset the customer by failing to recognize his or her specific situation.

Customer databases should be constructed to allow recording and updating of the complete customer roles and responsibilities, as well as their contribution to the relationship. All interactions, even if they are not monetary, should be recorded, to create a powerful account of who the customer is and what he or she stands for.

Customers who purchase small amounts, but influence others in their large purchases, should be recognized, flagged, and treated differently to ensure reinforcement of that behavior. Companies should collect and create fields in the database to keep a record of these people and recognize their issues. The complete relationship account should keep track of:

- Purchases
- Service issues and resolutions
- Unresolved issues
- Ideas submitted
- Circle of influence on other customers
- Referrals provided
- Focus group participation
- Survey contribution (including frequency)
- Complaints submitted
- Personal information (as legally permitted)
- Preferred magazines
- Preferred web sites
- Preferred hobbies

It is critical, of course, to do something with all the collected data and make them available to all your employees and all the different touch points. Collecting ideas and neglecting them is worse than not collecting at all. Your customer databases should be expanded to new fields—and reporting based on those fields—to allow you to isolate and identify trends, so you can then treat the true loyalists better and work on those who are not fully participating to identify issues and action plans.

Expanding the customer relationship account should empower your people to deliver more customized treatment and thus forge better relationships. It will also assist you in identifying the true loyalists, who often are not the biggest purchasers.

Our customers do not live in isolation. They are social creatures connecting to a social network. They create for themselves an ecosystem that accepts and respects them. That ecosystem consists of multiple components, including but not limited to family members, friends, web sites, work colleagues, and hobby buddies. The customer can be an influencer or an expert, sharing information with many others. They can be part of someone else's network, influenced by others. The ecosystem in which the customer lives (even including the magazines frequently read and the preferred web sites from which to draw opinions) is as critical to know as the color preference. It is within these ecosystems that customers make their preferences and selections. Whatever fits the ecosystem becomes a first-priority choice; fitting into the ecosystem ensures that the choice will not create conflict but will reinforce the ecosystem's supporting role. Products or services that are not an integral part of the ecosystem will be regarded as conflicting and therefore not desirable.

In attempting to be part of the customer ecosystem, companies invest in sponsoring and being associated with sports and music events; they also place their products in movies. Although these are good starting steps, they don't really reach customers or connect well with them.

In accordance with the theory of connectedness and people as parts of social networks, the expanded, holistic relationship accounts should reflect social aspects of the customer. Identifying these aspects and collecting ecosystem information allows you to communicate very personal, experience-based messages to customers and to relate to them within their ecosystem and not outside it. By doing so, you increase the chances of being regarded as an integral part of the ecosystem and thus a preferred product or service provider versus an outsider, who is in conflict with the ecosystem flow.

Krispy Kreme's[1] success was highly tied to their ability to integrate themselves into their customer ecosystem and become an integral part of it. The company participates in community events and contributes to them. Customers know that Krispy Kreme will always be at such events. The result is greater loyalty but also much lower costs of doing business by eliminating costly advertising. Community involvement spreads the word in a more genuine way, through satisfied customers, saving the cost of less credible marketing methods.

"Drink with commitment" and "Shake your conscience" are some of the leading slogans of a brand new cola drink. In a market in which Pepsi and Coca Cola have been dominating forces, a new entrepreneur has built a successful, although controversial, new business. Mecca Cola[2] is calling all Muslims to change their drinking habits and consume Mecca Cola over the leading global brand. The reason? Mecca Cola is committed to Muslim social causes and thus claims to deliver a completely different drinking experience.

Mr. Taufik Mathlouthi, the founder and president of Mecca Cola, created a concept that links drinking to the customer ecosystem. By assuming a religious connection, he is attempting to connect to his consumer on a higher experience level than simply fulfilling thirst, as other beverage vendors do. He is linking his products to the ecosystem of his consumers and forging a stronger bond through causes that matter to them.

Many experts will argue that any mixing of commercial and religious interests is a dangerous matter. It is probably true. But it might also be unavoidable. Religion is an important part of the customer's ecosystem. It is a sacred part as well. Learning to respect it and connect to it is a serious, unavoidable challenge for companies that want to be part of the customer's ecosystem. Mecca Cola is not alone. In Israel, cellular phone providers and car rental companies offer special deals to orthodox Jews who commit to avoid using their cell phones or rented cars over the Jewish Sabbath. Knowing that Orthodox Jews do not drive or answer phone calls on the Sabbath because of religious requirements, the vendors adapted themselves, demonstrated sensitivity, and customized their offering accordingly. It is this recognition of religious matters, which are an integral part of the customer's ecosystem, that allows those vendors to forge stronger bonds with their customers.

A similar approach can be found at Aveda,[3] the nature-based cosmetics and personal care products company. Aveda follows the environmentally correct mantra and connects well with consumers who care about such social responsibility. Acting out of its own convictions, Aveda connects them with the customer's concerns, which are part of the customer's ecosystem. Customers who care about the environment will find in Aveda a personal friend and, unlike the rest of the personal care suppliers, a colleague sharing the same social agenda—not just a purveyor of products. This is the essence of connecting to the customer's ecosystem and becoming a natural, integral part of it.

In all the cases mentioned above, there is one key ingredient to success: sincerity. Aveda, Mecca Cola, and Krispy Kreme did it because they personally believed in it. They shared the same value system as their customers. It is this sincerity that allowed them to connect on such a personal level. Companies that fake interest in the customer's ecosystem are bound to experience a boomerang effect. Customers will loathe them even more, stay away from their products, and spread the negative word about them. Participating in the customer ecosystem ought to be done with sensitivity and caring. This is a highly personal aspect of the customer, and it must be respected. Companies that participate in the ecosystem should do so on the customer's terms.

Achieving this level of intimacy and involvement in the customer's ecosystem is a privilege. It should be treated as such. This higher level of connection allows you to build a powerful differentiating tool that approaches the complete customer and not just his or her wallet. The more you know about your customers, the better your customization and execution. Going beyond the purchasing prism allows you to understand your customers better and treat them in a more personal way.

VISUALIZING VALUE

Many products and services are suffering from the commoditization plague. They simply are not appreciated by the customers who consume them. As an executive once told me, "At best I will not get customer complaints. But I no longer expect a thank you or appreciation." "Customers simply ignore our existence," he added. His products are suffering from unrecognized value. The customers simply do not see the value and usually interface with such companies through the problems they experience. For example, an Internet service provider will get upset comments for one hour of downtime, but never a thank-you note for the 99.9% of the time the service is operating flawlessly.

At the root cause of the problem is the company's responsibility to show customers the value they deliver. They need to create a set of tools and methods to ensure that customers never lose sight of the value delivered to them. Companies expect their customers to see the value on their own ("otherwise, why are they paying," they will argue). However, inertia-based customers simply do not bother looking for the value. They are busy focusing on other issues that matter to them, and they leave such services positioned in the well of commodity.

The need to value visualization methods is especially acute for industries such as technology, banking, insurance, telecom, and other utilities-type products and services. Customers will simply take ongoing operations for granted and will become active in the relationship only exceptionally, getting upset when the service is not flawless.

Companies will have to be creative and develop tools and visual methods to demonstrate the value of (sometimes) the most mundane products. If they want to be considered irreplaceable rather than interchangeable, the answer lies in creating value visualization tools. Rather than rushing to reduce value through cost reduction, visualizing value tools are a powerful way to combat commoditization.

Verizon: Cashing In on the Invisible

As prices were dropping fast in the wireless business, Verizon[4] was faced with a higher customer defection rate, lack of appreciation of value, and decreasing margins. The challenge was to create differentiation in customers' minds and become the preferred vendor, not a supplier of commodities. In fact, the real challenge was to create a way for customers to visualize unseen value.

The company decided to focus on its higher commitment to quality of coverage and service, leveraging its internal quality assurance team of employees, who drive specially equipped cars with multiple phones and who are constantly dialing to ensure Verizon's network superiority. To communicate this face, the company launched the famous "Can you hear me now?" advertising campaign, in which it shows a technical-looking person with a phone, traveling the country and constantly checking on his cell phone coverage by asking, "Can you hear me now?"

The campaign allowed the company to communicate the superior quality and provided customers with a visual way to see the value provided. As a result, Verizon's net customer base grew by 10% in 2002 to 32.5 million customers and by 15% in 2003 to 37.5 million customers. Reliability—and not price—became the key purchasing consideration. In addition, Verizon experienced margin improvements, while the campaign slogan became a pop-culture hit.

Continental Airlines: Accentuating the Positive

Recently, Continental[5] initiated a host of visualizing value activities under the theme of "Elite Access" for its premier customers. During check-in, the ticket kiosk or the web site will remind you that you are entitled to Elite Access treatment. Boarding passes are printed with Elite Access logos. During boarding, a special Elite Access line is available, with a special carpet and a sign differentiating premier customers from the rest of the pack. All these visuals create a clear way for the customers to visualize the value they are being provided and the preference bestowed upon them.

I often come across hotels and other service providers who skimp on visualizing value and provide the same key and items to both nonpremier and premier customers, in the name of efficiency. Instead of differentiating and visualizing the value, they actually dilute their premium value and create doubts in the customer's mind about whether the premium service is worth it. After all, it does *look* the same.

It is the role of the companies to develop reporting tools and other methods to demonstrate the ongoing value they deliver and ensure that customers appreciate it and see the exceptions in the context of those ongoing deliveries. The reasons for companies to invest in value visualization go beyond just being nice to customers. This is an effective tool to reduce customer churn rate and price deterioration. Customers who see the value do not go in search of other, cheaper vendors. In addition, customers who appreciate the value tend to complain with a different attitude. The cost of complaints drops, as the complaint intensity and cost of resolution drop because of a more reasonable and forgiving approach on the customer's part.

Visualizing value is important to the health of the relationship. It is never healthy for one side to take the other for granted. Each side must make the investment and ensure that the other side recognizes those efforts and appreciates them.

CULTURE OF EXCELLENCE

Excellence and quality are two of the most abused terms in corporate culture. Every company strives for them, but most do not really define them. Employees who are exposed to these abstract terms are often confused as to what is really expected from them.

Vision of Excellence

You may conduct this exercise with your direct reports. Ask your employees to close their eyes and imagine excellence. Then ask them to imagine quality and greatness. Then ask them to imagine a lemon. After they open their eyes, ask them to describe the images of excellence, quality, and greatness.

- What color were they?
- What shape were they?
- What did they look like?
- What size were they?

Most likely, each person will have a highly personal interpretation of these abstract concepts. When we conduct this exercise, we hear a wide variety of personal views equating excellence to climbing Mount Everest, a sunset, a Mexican beach, a child's smile, or a new Tiffany diamond necklace. When asked about the lemon, everyone produced the same description— the same color and the same shape.

The lesson of this exercise is this: abstract concepts like excellence and quality are subject to quite personal interpretations. Employees are convinced that they are already doing their best and exceeding expectations—because they adhere to *their* version of excellence. They deliver excellence as *they* see it. Their view is not necessarily consistent with your view. In addition, their view is often not consistent with the customers' views or expectations. When we recently conducted a gap analysis between employee and customer expectations for a division of a Fortune 500 company, we found that whereas 96% of the employees claimed they exceeded expectations, only 35% of the customers agreed with the same statement.

Leaving the excellence concept up to employee interpretation will guarantee inconsistency in service and often just ensure bad service. Under corporate efficiency pressures, employees develop a distorted and unsatisfying vision of service and experience excellence.

Organizations must take ownership of their cultures and be proactive about developing a concrete program to create and nurture a culture of real excellence. They must breathe life into those abstract concepts to ensure that employees follow their guidelines. First and foremost, they must encourage rule-breaking behavior and then collect and reward those stories. Then, incorporating those stories into the everyday culture and language of the company, they must transform the organization's culture into one that is excellence focused. The more stories you have, the richer and more attractive the culture. It is hero stories, as mentioned in the previous chapter, that create the soul of a company. It is a true source of passion and attraction that makes other employees want to follow and exceed them.

The Culture of Excellence Development Program should include the following components:

- Clear guidelines, values, and principles for the desired culture and the type of examples that represent excellence versus those that are just fulfilling a task.

- Ownership and sponsorship, so it is not something people do in their spare time, but an activity that has an executive dedicated to its development. This has to be a concentrated and proactive effort.

- Public recognition to reinforce the desirability of this behavior.

- Collection and publication of all excellence stories to ensure wide reach within the organization and customer base.

- Manager mentoring to ensure it will be reviewed and incorporated in all staff meetings.

- Visual reminders to employees and managers about culture development efforts and the existence of core values, as well as a call for action to execute them.
- Ongoing distribution of examples to all constituents.

The culture of excellence should not be treated as a program, which implies a starting point and an end, but rather as a way of living. *Commitment to excellence is a lifestyle choice, not a commercial choice.* Employees need to understand that excellence cannot be forced. Either they will want to be part of that culture and live by it, or they will not belong.

Culture development takes time. It is not a one-time launch activity, but a way of life. Cultures of nations form over decades and centuries. It will take time for your employees to absorb, accept, believe, and live by your new vision. Retaining and nurturing your culture of excellence beyond the initial launch is crucial to its life and success.

Creating tools and stories to allow employees to see an operational view of delivering excellence is at the heart of nurturing the culture of excellence. You must breathe life into your abstract intentions to unleash the power of your employees' passion.

Your customer experience and relationship, including its length and profitability, are highly dependent on employee experiences. The employee experience is dependent on your ability to create and nurture a culture of excellence.

Do we really care? Excellence is a matter of lifestyle choice. It is not just a commercial question. There are companies that get by without delivering excellence during the post-sales stage. But I doubt if you want to join them. They are fighting commoditization every day and face a downward spiral path.

Caring requires sincerity. Today's increasingly suspicious customer will examine your intentions more carefully than ever. If you make the choice to care, beyond the sale, then do it all the way. Put your passion behind it and demonstrate your true intentions for long-lasting relationships. Pass through all the key checkpoints such as rewarding customers and insight management. Create value visualization methods and demonstrate that you are doing your part. Manage the complete relationships account and connect to the customer's ecosystem.

Delivering excellence is hard work. That is why many companies fail in doing it. They would rather believe they can get away without it. You do not have to join this line of wishful thinkers. Commitment to caring and excellence is also a natural choice. The rewards are clear. For some companies, the sincere ones, it is the only choice.

Endnotes

1. Dominic Rushe, "Hole in One for Cult Doughnut" (London: *The Sunday Times*, September 21, 2003), Section 3, p. 6.

2. *www.Mecca-cola.com.*

3. *www.aveda.com.*

4. Scott Woolley, "Do You Fear Me Now?" (New York: *Forbes*, November 10, 2003), p. 78.

5. *www.continental.com.*

10

CRITICAL CHOICE 9: WHAT DO OUR MEASUREMENTS SAY ABOUT US?

In one of our consulting engagements, we were asked to audit and provide advice to the service and reservations center for one of the largest U.S. airlines. When we conduct such an audit, we always search for positive activities so that we can demonstrate success and recommend repeating it. In this way our recommendations are not just negative criticism. To achieve this goal, we approached the platinum line of the airline. This is a dedicated line for the airline's most valuable customers, people who fly at least 75,000 miles a year with the airline. By anybody's measure, including the airline's, these are people who should be treated royally.

To our surprise, we noticed that customers who are on hold for more than 59 minutes are hung up automatically by the center's switchboard. Since this is a rather long wait, I assumed that no one was affected by this bizarre rule. To my amazement, *every week* 400 platinum customers were subjected to this treatment.

When we presented our findings, we regarded the bizarre hang-up as a configuration error in the switchboard and recommended that it be fixed immediately. The airline's VP of customer service, however, insisted that it was not an error. In a closed-door meeting, after removing all his direct reports from the room, he claimed that he adjusts it every week. Every week, he told us, he checks the load and adjusts the automatic hang-up system. When the load is higher, the system is set to hang up on people after 25 and not 59 minutes. After inquiring about the reason for this behavior, he replied "That is what they are paying me for."

This VP, like many others, is being paid on the basis of his adherence to "average handling time," which consists of talk time *and* wait time in his center. If he goes above the target numbers, he loses part of his salary. When

163

he investigated the switchboard system, he realized that if the system is set to hang up automatically on people before they reach a live person, then the system does not register it as a call but rather as "an abandoned from hold" call, which means it looks like the customer's fault and not his. Thus he learned to tweak the system and make sure he meets his numbers, regardless. After all, his salary is tied to these numbers.

When confronted with the issue of upsetting the airline's most important and profitable customers, he plainly replied, "If it would have been important to the airline, they would have reflected it in my measurements." In a twisted way, he was right. He was doing what he was told and paid to do. It is the airline's responsibility to set the measurements correctly.

This behavior is no different in many other companies. Instead of the average handling time, productivity measurements prevail through other venues such as aggressive sales quotas with no regard to quality of sales, which often leads to deceptive methods and unacceptable commitment on behalf of the company. As discussed before, customer satisfaction surveys became another way to abuse the system and ensure more compensation than satisfaction. Questions and customers will be targeted in a way that will ensure the executive's pay, not the customer's complete satisfaction. As our CEM study indicated, over two-thirds of executives claim that their pay plan does not reflect commitment to quality of service, but rather productivity.

These and many other performance management numbers are distorting our vision of what truly matters to the customer and what truly measures the success of the relationship. These are self-serving numbers that usually address issues like market share and expansion plans, rather than increased competitiveness or value to customers.

This leads us to this critical choice. Do we pay people to please customers and delight them or to churn them? Employees follow the money trail. What they are paid to do is what they regard as the company's top goals. Therefore, you should examine the measurements you run the business by and ask yourself: in what way do they represent the relationships and experiences we are seeking?

ACTIONS, NOT PERCEPTION

Throughout the years, companies developed customer satisfaction measurement methods to pat themselves on the back. Customer satisfaction is geared toward measuring perceptions, not actions. The problem with perceptions is that you cannot take them to the bank. Customers will provide them easily, because it does not cost them much. Commitments for future purchases are something completely different, and they are difficult to obtain. Even though the state of affairs in every company includes some bragging rights about customer satisfaction improvements, the reality is completely different.

A Walker Information Walker Loyalty Report from July 2003 indicates that among customers of financial services companies, 75% of customers are satisfied but only 61% will rate service as excellent or very good:

- Only 41% see the value as excellent or very good.
- Only 34% plan to stay with their vendor (despite satisfaction).
- 42% are not switching because of the inertia, time, and effort associated with a switch.
- Only 16% said they would not consider a competitive offer.
- 55% believe their vendor cares about their customers.

I am confident that many of these banks and brokers have surveys to demonstrate satisfaction in the mid-90% range, but the reality is different. If only 16% of our satisfied customers would not consider a competitive offer, we are facing a serious challenge.

To truly reflect the customer view, companies must shift from perceptions to actions. Measurements should examine customer actions such as increases in overall value and purchasing. Margin increases and thank-you letters, as well as referrals, are all action-based measurements that go beyond perceptions. It is easier to measure perception because the customer does not have to commit to anything. Actions, however, are taken more seriously by customers.

MEASURING SUCCESS: THE CUSTOMER STYLE

The purpose of shifting from a products/service strategy to a customer-centric strategy must be well documented, with specific business results. This is not an exercise in being nicer. It is a strategy to maximize revenues through better, more meaningful relationships with customers.

Every company has a different set of desired business results, based on its competitive advantages and current market positioning. While one company will seek to extend the average customer life cycle, another will look at reducing the cost of post-sales service as the key driver for the strategy. Market leaders may choose to emphasize continuing leadership through the customer-centric strategy, whereas niche players will seek to enhance their niche position and add more value to niche-seeking customers. While developing these financial/business objectives, every company must benchmark those targets that must be established for the purposes of comparison and measuring the progress and results of the strategy.

Customer-centric strategies deliver both cost reduction *and* new revenue streams. Employee turnover and customer churn rates are often cost-based reasons to launch a customer-centric strategy. However, some companies will seek to gain more sales per customer as the key driver for launching the strategy.

As we are examining our measurements and moving toward customer action-based factors, we ought to consider the financial impact of customer strategies on the overall business. After all, it is exactly those customer actions that will drive the justification for the customer strategy and its associated costs. The factors to be considered are divided into cost-based and revenue-based categories:

- Cost-Based Factors
  - Shortened sales cycle
  - Lower cost of sales
  - Lower cost of marketing
  - Higher marketing accuracy
  - Reduction in customer-service costs
  - Reduction in customer defections
  - Increase in inventory utilization
  - Reduction in cost of hiring
  - Reduction in cost of training
  - Reduction in cost of employee turnover

- Revenue-Based Factors
  - Increase in sales size per customer
  - Increase in overall wallet share
  - Increase in annual value
  - Increase in referrals
  - Increase in length of relationship
  - Increase in penetration per geography
  - Increase in profit margins
  - Increase in cross-sells
  - Increase in up-sells
  - Increase in sales force effectiveness

All these factors represent actions that the customer took to support our business and deepen his or her commitment to us. A sales cycle reduction implies that the customer trusts us more and is willing to accept our new products faster. An increase in annual value implies increased spending with our company, instead of the competition.

MEASUREMENT GUIDELINES

When developing your financial model to justify the strategy, consider the following guidelines:

- The strategy for customer-centric financial objectives should not come at the expense of effectiveness. Implementing a customer-centric strategy is not a license to lose all the benefits of a well-established operation. The strategy needs to leverage those benefits and build on top of them.
- Operational effectiveness is an important measure, but it has to be developed in the light of customer-centric activities and not in isolation.
- When customer-centric objectives and operational effectiveness objectives are in conflict, customer-centric objectives must take precedence. After all, the customer is the reason for the company's existence.

IDENTIFYING BUSINESS DRIVERS

List five business objectives that should justify developing and implementing a customer-centric strategy in your company. Consider your own market dynamics, competitive landscape, and business model with your customers when listing those objectives. After you've set these objectives, assess the improvement required in each objective and the way you plan to measure progress and improvements.

Objective	Desired Improvement	Current Measurement

For many customer-centric companies, this complex process is consolidated into one single factor: "Would you recommend us to someone else?" They truly believe that when customers venture into the domain of willingness to recommend, they are lending the company their own credibility. This credibility is the highest form of recognition and appreciation. When customers want to lend you their reputation, it indicates true success and satisfaction beyond any doubt.

Enterprise Rent-a-Car[1] uses such a method to measure its branches' success and performance. Employee promotions and pay are tied to this single question, which determines the success of the company overall. By simplifying the measurements, they achieve clearer focus and a commitment of employees to the highest level of service. They also avoid the typical trap in which everyone is meeting their numbers but the customer is upset — a trap often seen when everyone looks after their own piece of the action, but no one is minding the total value proposition.

During a visit to a health care insurance company named David Shield, I discovered a surprising compensation plan. It is not one of the largest in the market, but some of its practices are admirable and ought to be copied. I was especially impressed by the company practice around employee accountability for customer issues. Employee compensation is not based on traditional salary and bonuses. It is rather based on customer issues. Every customer service employee is paid based on the number of customer requests and complaints he or she handles. The moment an employee receives a customer request, it is logged with him or her as the sole owner of the problem. Delegation to someone else in the organization is not permitted. Every employee is held responsible to resolve the customer issues he or she receives and do so within a certain time frame. The compensation plan is directly linked to the number of issues resolved by each employee. The company regularly tracks all employees' performance and compensates them accordingly. In addition, if a certain problem is not resolved within the allocated time, the employee will face a financial penalty, which is deducted from the paycheck. If the customer called again regarding the same issue, another penalty will be applied to the employee's salary.

For some this policy may sound a bit harsh. But the business of ensuring ownership responsibility and accountability is a powerful tool. This compensation scheme ensures that no customer issue will be left behind or fall between the cracks. There is no handing over to anyone else or delegation of responsibility, as is commonly done in many base-salary type organizations. In such a compensation plan, you do not need to depend on customer satisfaction to determine success. The ultimate success is determined by the reduction in repeat calls for the same issue. A customer action and not a perception determines the company's success and therefore its compensation plan.

The compensation plan is a litmus test for companies' seriousness about their customer strategies. It is when executives and companies put their money where their mouth is. It is the ultimate adjustment of performance measurements. It is the test every organization must pass about their commitment to customer strategies.

TRUE ASSETS

"Whatever you can measure you can manage. And whatever you cannot measure, you cannot manage." This corporate mantra is leading many executives to live or die by their pie charts and graphs. They become slaves of the reports and the numbers, forcing everything to fit this narrow prism.

In reality, whatever you can measure, someone else can manage better. If it is all a numbers game, your competition will always find a way to cut costs. You cannot out-save your competition, so this is not a long-term strategy.

When Ken Kutaragi fought for his project, his CEO was reluctant. The CEO did not believe the project would bring the promised results. At a certain point, he prohibited Ken from investing any more effort. It was Ken's conviction and courage that made him continue the project, under the CEO's radar, in a small office complex at the outskirts of the city. In 2003, 50% of Sony's profits came from Ken's forbidden project, also known as PlayStation 2. How would you measure that?

Ken Kutaragi eventually became the president of Sony's division that manages all the play station business.

Every company's success is highly dependent on a set of assets that cannot be fitted into a pie chart, and yet they are alive and influential. How would one measure risk taking, leadership, courage, commitment, innovation, caring, and sincerity? These are highly critical assets, yet they do not fit into any graph. Does that mean they do not exist or make an impact? Not only do they exist and make an impact, they are probably more critical to the company's success than the things being measured.

In the early 1990s, envying Southwest's success, both United Airlines and Continental Airlines decided to form no-frills competitors. Both launched low-cost airlines to compete with and beat Southwest, which had started to make a dent in their backyards. They copied, exactly, the highly acclaimed operational excellence of Southwest and managed to squeeze in one more daily flight, just as Southwest did, from every airplane. It seemed they were destined for success. Instead, both ventures folded after great losses in less than two years, while Southwest continues its profitable success.

United and Continental made the grave mistake of "whatever you can measure you can manage." They assumed that by copying Southwest's legendary operation, they would be able to beat them. But for Southwest it was never an operational game. Unlike its competitors, Southwest recognized and nurtured its true assets, its people and customers. Led by its CEO at the time, Herb Kelleher, Southwest realized that the assets they cannot measure are the ones that matter. Thus they built a system that nurtured those assets and made it a fun place for their employees, who, in return, made the airline the fun airline to fly. While Southwest minded the employee experience, the employees, in return, minded the customer experience.

From Valentine's Day cards to fun signing of security instructions, the company was constantly reinventing employee experiences and bestowing on them the power to resolve problems right away. When Southwest was sued over a slogan infringement, Mr. Kelleher called the suing company's CEO and asked him to resolve the matter outside of court. He did not have arbitration in mind. Instead, he offered to arm-wrestle the competitor for the slogan. Upon obtaining an agreement, Mr. Kelleher arranged a large arena and invited the press for the party. It became a huge PR success for the company, even though Mr. Kelleher lost the wrestling competition.

But the message to all the employees was a huge triumph for him. The message was, "We do not drag out disputes. We take care of them quickly and with minimum hassle." No amount of training could have delivered this message as effectively as the competition he staged. He was a role model for the company's principles.

NURTURING RATHER THAN MANAGING

Every organization measures itself by the assets it owns—buildings, money in the bank, equipment, and other material assets. But every company has a set of intangible assets. Some will consider the brand and customer base and other intangibles as additional assets. Innovative measurements tools were invented to capture their value. The true assets of each business, however, are its people. Their attitude, caring, risk taking, decision-making, courage, leadership, innovation, and inspiration are some of those true assets. They cannot be fully measured and accounted for. No balance sheet can contain them. The true assets cannot be managed. No compensation can force performance from employees. Yet they are critical to the company's success. They are the secret sauce of the winning companies, while their competition is struggling to catch up with the operational numbers.

At the core of every company is an internal experience that determines the behavior of its people. This is the DNA that sets the execution level of all the other true assets. A great experience will unleash the best in your employees; with bad experiences, they will become reserved and restricted, and they will do the very minimum required to survive.

Innovating and leading, taking risks, and acting with care are employee choices. If nurtured correctly, a supportive experience environment will evolve in which employees will participate willingly. They will not do so if they will be considered outcasts, suckers, or unappreciated peons. Employees need to see that the corporate ecosystem is supportive of this type of behavior, and *then* they will join the program.

From role modeling, to recognition of employees who took risks, to examples from the outside world, companies can build such an ecosystem, an ecosystem that will bring out the best in its employees. Expecting employees to care or innovate is asking them to become emotionally bonded to the company. This is not a simple request, and companies should be ready to reciprocate. Although emotions don't fit well in the corporate pie chart, they are alive and kicking. The question is: will they kick in your organization or kick you elsewhere? Would employees care to give you their emotional commitment or would they reserve it for outside activities—or maybe the competition to whom they plan to defect?

We try to tap into emotions. We ought to recognize them and get ready for them.

Achieving that will require companies first to recognize their true assets and then to prioritize their nourishment. They must demonstrate true appreciation of emotions and not just number-crunching efficiency. Employees easily reserve their emotional commitment, fearing ridicule and lack of appreciation. Companies must demonstrate to their employees that those emotional commitments are not the exception, but rather the rule. They are the modus operandi the company is seeking.

To do so, it must move beyond the self-serving quarterly targets and make the choice to support customer actions. This is the first step toward signaling to employees that customers are truly important and that the company is honest about its intentions. This trust-building effort, with honest execution, will send a clear message to employees—a message that a true partnership exists and that appreciation will be given to those who demonstrate commitment. It is exactly this type of emotional bond that unleashes the true assets of the company.

Making the performance and measurement choice requires another fundamental change. The customer cannot be one of many items on the measurements list. It ought to be *the* list. As discussed, there are many customer actions that can demonstrate a good job is being done. They also provide the financial justification for becoming customer focused. It is by shifting customer behavior, not perceptions, that companies can be assured that they are building true relationships. Customers demonstrate their commitment through actions, not perceptions.

Making the measurements choice is about being sincere and true to yourself. It is about aligning the intentions with the results. It is going beyond listening to customers and adjusting a few features accordingly. It is about measuring your success purely from the customer perspective. Making this choice will require humility and truthfulness. But it is probably the most challenging choice.

Endnote

1. Frederick S. Reichheld, "The One Number You Need to Grow" (Cambridge: *Harvard Business Review,* December 2003).

11

CRITICAL CHOICE 10: HOW LONG DO WE MILK OUR PRODUCTS?

As the gavel hit the table, the audience was shocked by the final price. The nose-piece, which was originally estimated at 10,000 euros, was sold for approximately $500,000 (approximately 450,000 euros). It was not the only item in this Paris auction that managed to command more than 20 times the asking price. The biggest surprise, however, came from the owners, who could not believe that more than $3 million had been generated by this charity auction.

Both Air France and British Airways offered pieces of their famous Concorde[1] for sale in November 2003. The auction, geared toward the support of local charities, followed the shutdown of Concorde service. To the owners' amazement, thousands of people came to the showing, and the auction proceeds beat all expectations. The joke went around that the Concorde was probably more profitable in pieces than as a whole airplane. What was amazing to the executives of Air France and British Airways was the amount of passion and love exhibited by those who came to the auction, and even those who didn't come. Dedicated web sites suddenly appeared, catering to Concorde aficionados, selling a wide variety of memorabilia.

The passion and commitment demonstrated a strong following, yet the Concorde could not generate sufficient revenues to support its regularly scheduled flights. How does one explain the discrepancy—passionate loyalists willing to pay for pieces of the experience on the one hand, but a decreasing number of passengers on the other? The answer is the critical choice that both airlines failed to make.

In the early 1970s, when the Concorde was launched, it was an attractive experience. It represented the jet set, glamour, and *the* place to be. Its technology was cutting edge and the appeal of breaking the sound barrier and making it to New York earlier than the time you departed meant a great deal to the people who were willing to pay for this premium experience. As time passed, the environment around the Concorde changed. Business and first class improved dramatically at other airlines. New technologies in aviation transformed the experiences of other airplanes, and new competitors such as Virgin Atlantic arrived, changing the rules of luxury and glamour. Yet the Concorde experience hardly changed. Both airlines decided to milk this product for all it was worth, without making *any* significant advancement in the airplane and its total experience.

Eventually, loyal passengers defected to newer, more appealing experiences, leaving the Concorde with fewer passengers and lower revenues. By the time the airlines decided to do something, it was too late. They fell into the success trap, believing it would last forever without the need for further investment. This is the typical trap faced by a company that reaches success and tries to ride it for all it's worth, maximizing its revenues and margins.

The choice and timing of innovation is critical for the relevance and freshness of experiences. Today's customers have an ever-decreasing tolerance for boring products and services. They are constantly tempted with new products and services, with a much greater selection to fill any void. Therefore, companies must crank up the innovation machine and decrease innovation time. The days of milking our products for all they are worth are long gone.

If you have ever encountered HP printers, you know that the company has an almost infinite number of versions—or at least it feels this way. HP made an early strategic decision not to let any other company cannibalize its products. So HP decided to cannibalize itself. By introducing a new version every six months and retiring the old version, its experience is kept fresh and relevant. HP might not pull the last dollar (which is usually the most expensive) out of each of their printers, but it managed to build a strong market position with both premium pricing and recurring revenues from accessories. This company succeeded because it chose innovation over milking the products for all they're worth over several years. For HP, innovation was the rule, not the exception, what it does every day, not what it does after getting stuck in the commoditization rut.

CONSISTENCY IS BORING

Consistency is a great way to lose customers fast. Unless you provide waste management, after a certain period customers will become bored by your consistent service and the excitement urge will creep in. If you don't provide it, they will seek it elsewhere.

Although originally consistency was necessary to ensure that customer expectations were met, today consistency serves a different purpose in many industries, that of an efficiency tool. It becomes a method of reducing costs by shrinking the work of all employees into one unified process; there is no diversion in execution. We sometimes call it an economy of scale. Economies of scale are about commoditizing our services and experiences. All customers are treated the same, as we perceive this behavior to be cheaper. This is the way successful companies fall into the trap and make a 180-degree turn, back to the problems they used to have that were caused by efficiency models and the efficient relationship paradox.

Of course, if your industry is plagued by inconsistency and bad reputations for inaccurate billing, for example, make sure that consistency is your first priority. But you should know that soon consistency will not register as a differentiator on the customer's radar screen and thus will not command premium price, preference, or permanence of relationship.

Excitement is the name of the game. Customers want variations and surprises. They do not want to feel stuck or taken for granted or that they are not making progress—all these are byproducts of consistency. "Keep me excited and I will have no reason to leave," your customer is saying. Unlike wine, experiences do not get better with time. They cannot stay static. They are dynamic, just like the people who are consuming and paying for them. They must evolve or decline; staying still is not healthy for them. So why aren't companies evolving their experiences?

SUCCESS BREEDS COMPLACENCY

First success happens. Companies quickly get used to it and believe in it. Executives tend to think that success is forever. After all, they worked hard for it. When success happens, they lose their natural paranoia that brought them to a successful state. They get comfortable and start believing that the growth line will continue to rise. They are sitting on their laurels. In short, they are making all the mistakes they know very well they shouldn't make.

Expanding Away

Another common mistake often associated with success is the expansion trap. Instead of focusing on the customers they succeeded in forging great relationships with, companies start expanding elsewhere, outside their core competence, neglecting their loyal customers in the process. These expansions take mindshare and attention away from nurturing success, as every executive is now busy with the new expansion plans, and no one is left to mind the shop.

Usually a fearless startup with nothing to lose will create disruption in the industry that will shake up the complacency. Another wakeup call often arises from major losses in the expansion venture that forces companies back to minding their experiences and customers. As mentioned before, Abbey wrote off $100 billion in losses before it returned to basics.

Commoditization Rut

Companies often assume that their industry reaches a commoditization stage, with price the only differentiator, naturally, after their successes and the appearance of competitors. Then discounting is the way to reach customers' attention. "Ours is a mature, tired market" they will claim. It might be the truth, but it represents executive laziness, not customer tiredness. Managers become complacent and tired and prefer not to take the big risks associated with innovation. Cutting costs and reducing prices seem to be easier, more predictable tasks. It is also the fast lane to extinction, but most executives prefer to ignore this fact.

The commoditization rut is a state of mind, one in which industry executives are not willing to take their business to the next level or are too afraid or embarrassed to ask for help. For every mature market story I hear, I think about JetBlue, Amazon.com, and Dell, all of which gave their industry a kick, while changing the rules and creating a great new business in someone else's mature market.

Reinvention Process

Disney Corporation[2] recently announced a new program to update Mickey Mouse. The 75-year-old mouse had apparently lost appeal with his core customers. Hardly updated during his lifetime, Mickey seemed to have lost his appeal to children because he did not fool around on computers, play with skateboards, or do the things that children do. Mickey simply lost touch with his audience. In short, he lost *relevance*. Just as with any other success, Disney focused on retaining it, not reinventing it. Disney perceived success as a destination, not a journey, and moved to maximize revenues from the existing experience. Efficiency took over.

Now Disney is facing a double challenge. One is the need to reinvent Mickey and create a relevant experience for today's kids. Assuming they are successful, they still have to face the second challenge, which is overcoming the replacement that children have selected over Mickey in the meantime.

When companies let their experience get stale and boring, customers go elsewhere. They do not sit and wait. They will get their adrenaline shot and excitement from other sources. When companies finally realize their mistakes, it is usually too late. Fixing the experience becomes the easy part of the task, while fighting new competitors makes success more difficult. Bringing back customers who defected to more exciting pastures (i.e., competitors) is difficult, costly, and often unsuccessful.

Companies must establish a quarterly review of their experiences, which should include evaluation of all internal and external aspects, such as:

- Competitive moves
- Change in customer preferences and budget availability
- Change in technology
- Change in sales and service channels

In mapping all these changes, they must examine the opportunities and threats associated with those changes and answer an important set of questions:

- How relevant is our experience?
- What does each of these changes mean to our experiences?
- What else can we do to take our experience to the next level?
- If we were a brand new player with no precedence or limitation, what would we have done?

The choices facing each company during the reinvention process are to:

- *Nurture.* Small incremental changes should be made to ensure that the experience will not become stale and boring and will keep customers excited and connected.
- *Grow.* After several incremental changes have been made, it is time to move to the next stage. You are probably seeing the commodity run on the horizon. A few customers have started a migration process by minimizing business with you and testing other options. Better act fast and avoid defection. It is time to take it to the next exciting level. Incremental changes will not suffice here. You must present a newer, improved experience that will reconnect customers to you.
- *Reinvent.* You probably missed the signs or you should not have been in this stage. It might be that big changes occurred fast, before you

had a chance to respond. This is the time for a major overhaul. It seems as if your experience lost touch with its core customers and it is time to put a strongly different experience in front of them, hoping they will come back. You may also choose here to appeal to a different customer base, but that too will require adaptations to the experience. Either way, it is time to put on your thinking cap, play with your Imagineering toys, and get a brand new experience out.

The reinventing process ensures that success does not affect you in the wrong way, that it does not send you into the so-easy-to-fall-into comfortable feeling that the customers will always be there and success is forever. You must retain the paranoia and keep on your toes, so as not to lose your success. Success is not a destination, but a journey. Remember that when you are successful, you also gather new competitors who watch your success and want a piece of it. During successful stages your paranoia needs to be on high alert.

For example, Krispy Kreme will need to consider people's growing concern with carbohydrates. This company will need to explore how it can match the change in customer eating habits. This type of customer change is an example of the need to conduct regular assessments of experience relevance.

Selections and prices are wider today than they have ever been; customers are in the driver's seat and they can push you out of the car sooner than you imagine, leaving you with high, unrealized investment. If only for the purpose of protecting your investment, make sure the experience does not get boring.

INNOVATION COMPASS: "WOW ME NOW"

There comes a time when connection with the customer is no longer sufficient. Customers can provide limited ideas and insights based on their limited practical view. They may compare your product with that of the competition and propose ways to improve it. They may address a current immediate need, but they will not think out-of-the-box for you. They do not have the foresight or depth of knowledge to come up with order-of-magnitude leaps and innovations. In fact, customers can assist companies with incremental improvement, but not with major innovation.

Counting too much on the customer for incremental insight and improvement can create a trap. The *Now* trap distorts your view from the bigger potential out there. You become trapped in fixing the Now for the customer, so you miss the next big *Wow*. In the meantime, while you are busy doing incremental work and expecting it to be satisfactory, your competition is forging a new leap, a brand new, exciting Wow.

Companies must learn how to manage their innovation compass. They must work both the Now and the Wow aspects and create a healthy balance that ensures they do not simply provide customers with what they expect, but also imagine the next big Wow they will bring to the relationship. The next big Wow will ensure that the customer perceives them as innovative, invested in the future, not just in quick wins, and interested in the relationship's longevity.

The Innovation Compass depicted in Exhibit 11.1 allows you to measure your status based on your respective quadrant. Focusing on the Wow process, startups are barely engaged with customers and envision something that does not exist. Many products, from the minivan to the Walkman, were not envisioned by customers but were actually rejected by them as unnecessary. It was only later that customers accepted the innovation and responded warmly. In 2004 Sony was celebrating 25 years of the Walkman, the product that was rejected during customer focus groups, the one that because of Sony's conviction created a brand new market segment and became a huge best seller with more than 300 million units sold in the first 25 years.

Exhibit 11.1   Innovation Compass

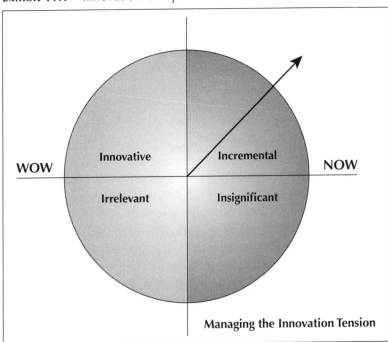

During the Wow stage, you are working with limited information and assurance and the risk is greater—but so is the potential reward.

During the Now stage, you are working incrementally, listening to your customers and then responding with improvements. This process has a high level of information and assurance, since we have high engagement with customers. The risk is lower and the reward is usually smaller. The incremental improvements we make hardly generate a significant increase in business. Instead, they retain the current level of business with customers while creating a few small bumps in the revenue.

Companies that fall below the Now level stop listening to their customers. Instead, they focus on their own cost-crunching operations. They often sink to the insignificant stage. In losing touch with customers and not creating the next Wow, they are accelerating their commoditization and minimizing their role and competitive position in their market. Most companies do not think they are in this stage, but focusing on costs and efficiency instead of customers brings them there faster than they think or want to believe. They usually wake up one day and discover their insignificance. Where were they until now? Busy cutting costs and not inventing.

From the insignificant stage, the path to irrelevance is almost ensured. Few companies manage to climb back up to the Wow or the Now stage. It is possible, but it requires a great deal of change, in both mind set and practice—change that most executives are too demoralized to pull off. They would rather be in denial and try to defend their position. By doing so, they put the last nail in their coffin. They become irrelevant. At this stage, their product plays an increasingly marginal role as the cost leader at the discount shops. They got what they wanted, but it came with a price. They became efficient enough to lose relevance with the customers completely.

Deliver the Now While Creating the Future Wow

The fine balancing act of living in both the Now and the Wow is what signifies successful, customer-centric companies. They constantly mind the experience in both of its aspects: the incremental and the innovative. They do not let success blind them, but rather understand that success draws more attention and thus creates a greater level of risk. Instead of sitting on their laurels, they examine the experience the company delivers ever more carefully and with greater paranoia to ensure that they never lose touch with their customers.

They refuse to take the customer for granted and they commit to work harder to ensure that the courting stage is never over. In a sense, they always stay in love, never accepting the marriage as a destination, but rather a reward that needs to be earned every day. Every day they earn their customer's loyalty, one experience at a time. Demonstrating their commitment, they listen and act on customer insights and then they go back to the drawing board, seeking insight beyond the incremental. They must stay relevant—and innovation is the road to it.

Endnotes

1. Kim Willsher, "Bidding Breaks Sound Barrier as Planespotters Swoop for Concorde Memorabilia" (London: *The Sunday Telegraph,* November 16, 2003), p. 18.
2. Oliver Poole, "Mixed-Up Mickey Gets a Makeover at 75" (London: *The Daily Telegraph,* November 19, 2003), p. 15.

12

THE ULTIMATE CHOICE:
CUSTOMER STRATEGIES—
A MUTUAL LIFETIME COMMITMENT

Eleven choices were detailed in previous chapters. Now we come to the ultimate choice: building long-term, mutual relationships—not relationships that will be measured by quick quarterly returns, but by long, profitable association.

It seems like common sense, so why is it listed as a choice? Just like the other choices we've discussed, on the surface it seems like a no-brainer. But when we examine the operational and strategic aspects, and measure the consequences and the price associated with it, we often become reluctant to act. So it joins the long list of beautiful choices that never saw the light of day.

As Exhibit 12.1 indicates, making the choice to become customer focused implies multiple choices and a different way of operating a business. From the people hired, to the experience delivered, through compensation and training, customer-centric companies are inherently different from product-centric companies. Each and every one of those choices is a testimony to the kind of company you are really running. The differences, as Exhibit 12.1 indicates, go far beyond semantics and statements. They are operational differences that lead companies to stronger, more passionate and profitable relationships with customers. It is these operational differences that set the winners apart from the dreamers. The ability to translate great intentions into actions and the courage to drive fundamental change—these are what is required to become truly customer focused and drive the business from the customer perspective.

STOP STARING

For years, we have been searching for the right formula for customer relationship success. We listened to the gurus and bought the books. We were

Exhibit 12.1 Visualizing the Difference

Product-Based Corporation	Function	Experience-Based Corporation
Obedient, rules-following people	Recruitment	Empowered, common-sense people
Procedures, rules, approval processes	Training and Tools	Principles, examples, and commercial judgment
Follow the rules	Performance Evaluation	Break the rules
Brand development, self-centric, awareness, and exposure	Marketing Focus	Experience-centric, creating a customer experience
Customer acquisition, product selling, "sell & run"	Sales Focus	Delivering an experience, relationship selling, "sell & stay"
Sales and rules adherence	Compensation	Exceeding customer expectations, customers' longevity
Nice to have. What experience?	Customers' Experience	At the core of all activities
Be happy you have a job	Employees' Experience	Acting on a mission

fascinated by the Ritz Carlton service commitment. We were jealous of the employees at Southwest for the fun environment in which they work. Secretly, we even fantasized about how we could change our own workplace. We craved the Starbucks customer commitment and rushed to buy a designed coffee such as venti caramel macchiato just to get the *taste* of that fabulous customer commitment. The stories of Disney and the geek squads inspired us, and we were ready to turn the world upside down for customers. But we didn't.

What went wrong? Why is it that we keep on participating in all these conferences, listening to all these speeches, eagerly swallowing all the stories, and yet nothing happens? We have plenty of financial and qualitative evidence to justify a better commitment to customers, and still nothing happens. We are simply staring, but not acting.

I would argue that beneath the surface are bigger issues preventing us from acting. It is not lack of knowledge or examples. Other companies took the risk and jumped into the cold water before us. These pioneering companies made the mistakes and fine-tuned the approach that would help us to avoid many of the pitfalls. They also reaped the benefits in a big way. And we kept on staring.

We did not act for various reasons (not through lack of ideas). Acting requires recognizing and addressing these issues:

- *Fear of Change.* Many of us are comfortable enough to keep the system operating the way it is. Change is often intimidating and causes internal resistance. Despite the inspiration, we did not gather enough strength to actually move our ideas to the action zone. Our perceived internal obstacles seem more powerful than our perceived ability to execute.

- *Immediate Dismissal.* We do not want to give the change a real chance in our own organization, fearing failure and ridicule. We have been there before; we have seen others easily and cynically dismissed for bringing up new ideas. "This is not how we do things here" was the response. Thus we actually tell *ourselves* why an idea will not work. We *become* the immediate dismissal we fear so much.

- *Size Matters.* We often believe the challenge is too large an undertaking, with risks that are too big. "I am too low/small in the organization to do it; this is the CEO's job," we comfort ourselves, as we let the inspiration of the story of the week wane. In reality, we are as small as we want ourselves to be.

- *Fake Humility.* "No one listens to me anyway," we often convince ourselves. In an amazing acceptance of the virtue of humility (temporarily, though), we drive home the message to ourselves that we are just not the type for such a challenge. We are not the type of champions to change the world. We are not made of legend material.

- *Too Big/Too Bureaucratic/Too Whatever.* Our organizations, we are convinced, are not made for such a change. "Customer individuality is for small and nimble companies," we want to believe, again spinning our refusal to drive change in large companies.

In reality, there is a bit of truth in each of these arguments; however, this piece of truth does not negate the fact that these are all excuses even *we* refuse to fully accept. It is time to stop staring. My favorite line is "no one ever erected a statue in honor of a committee." Individuals with courage and conviction *make* the majority that drives change. This is a choice you must make. No one can make it for you. Either you will embrace the challenge or you will leave it to others. The last thing you want to see happen is one of your peers deciding to be that majority of one who will drive this change and reap the rewards. Stop staring. Start acting. You know it is the right thing to do. You know it will make the right impact on the company. You know it is something you will enjoy doing. It comes from a place where you are very passionate. Stop staring at your own passion. Make it happen.

COMPLETE VIEW OF A SUCCESSFUL CUSTOMER STRATEGY

To succeed in making it happen, you must start with a clear vision in mind. You should be able to see the smiling, surprised faces of your customers as they experience your newly designed experiences. You must envision a clear segmentation process that focuses on the right customers, while neglecting the ones that are not suitable for you.

You also must define a clear financial justification for the efforts. Change is not free. It will require investment to change processes, educate people, and acquire the tools. You ought to know and document why you are putting forth all these efforts. As detailed before, there are many financial drivers that justify customer strategies, so you should create a customized plan and be ready to measure and execute it. If you execute it well, you are most likely to exceed expectations and see customers showering you with loyalty and new business.

It is a strategy after all—nothing less. A program or initiative is most likely to join the rest of the failing ones preceding it. The customer is ever more suspicious and will not be fooled easily. So you must be ready to provide complete commitment or not bother at all. Do not settle for less, or it is most likely to backfire. The customer's past bad experiences will lead to greater resentment, especially if you repeat the mistakes of your competitors when they overpromise and underdeliver.

Look at the complete picture, including all the choices to which you must commit, and make sure they are backed by a detailed action plan. To implement your plan successfully, recognize what you give up. List all the practices that must be changed. Recognize that in order for the new to be allowed, some of the old must go. Attempting to build your customer strategy on top of your old efficiency model is a sure path to failure.

ORGANIZATIONAL COMMITMENT

It takes champions with courage to make things happen or change the world, but it takes a whole organization to execute a change. Avoid the pitfall of the silo-focused, hierarchy-based organization, and engage the whole organization in the ownership and execution process.

You must obtain an organizational commitment to make your strategy operational.

Every part of the business must know and own its part of the experience, and everyone must be measured and compensated on the basis of their own portions, as well as the overall customer action-based objectives. Tying the strategy to compensation and measurements is the way to send a clear message about the staying power of the strategy and encourage employees to go through with the changes required. They will be reluctant at first, suspiciously examining the importance and seriousness of the new strategy. Show them that you mean business. Go beyond the memo and the T-shirt. Hard-code your strategy in the operation of the business to ensure that employees cannot and will not avoid it.

CHANGE THE RULES THROUGH AMAZING EXPERIENCES

Customer experiences are not about being nice to customers. They are about loving customers and making money in the process—a *lot* of money. They represent not just another incremental increase, but order-of-magnitude differentiation.

Great experiences change the rules of the industry. They set you apart from the pack. While everyone else is focusing on efficient transactions, you are tapping into the emotions and aspirations of your customers and creating a powerful connection with them through powerful experiences. It is the way to break the rules, try something new, and charge far more for it.

So stop following the crowd. Following market trends is about following someone else's agenda. The likelihood is that by doing so, you will fulfill someone else's agenda and barely enjoy the few unprofitable crumbs left for you by the leader.

I recently learned this lesson in a most unexpected way. As I was landing at Reagan Airport, I was picked up by an SUV taxi. The driver, who was also the owner, had installed massage devices in the passenger seats. The massage service was free of charge to all passengers, who were able to select their type and strength of massage. The driver provided this service free of charge and was happy to see his customers enjoying it. Understanding the customer experience, he knew very well the feelings of a person just off the plane rushing to a meeting with a stiff neck and a backache. To be in top shape for your important meeting, you had better get rid of your aches and pains, but time is scarce, so you just let them linger and distract you. Our massage taxi driver decided to change the rules and align his value with the customer experience. He did not follow the rules of taxis as commodities. He did not read the industry's publications, which would have guided him on how to squeeze customers for more money. He simply put himself in the shoes of the customer, imagined the experience, and then went ahead and responded to it.

Needless to say, I used the service, enjoyed it, and tipped him handsomely. It was worth it. He surprised me and pleased me—and solved a real problem. For that I was willing to pay more. He was smart *not* to put a price tag on the new massage experience, but to provide it for free. If there had been a price, most of the passengers would have skipped the massage. This way, everyone used it, without exception, the driver told me. As for the pay, they all paid him more in tips than he could imagine charging for a massage. The value in the passengers' eyes was much greater, as it usually is with great experiences, than a middle-of-the-road price would have been.

When I asked him whether he could pick me up on the way back to the airport, he said he was already fully booked in the afternoon. I wasn't surprised. Usually rule-breakers who invent new experiences are "suffering" from high demand and repeat business.

Be your own leader. Through experiences, you can change the rules. You are actually expected to do it. You chart your own new path and force the competition to follow. And if you do your job well and do not succumb to success (while your competition scrambles to figure out how you changed the rules and how to match the new ones), you will be busy creating even newer rules.

This is the ultimate choice: you can either lead, through powerful, unique, and personalized experience, follow the leader of the efficiency model, or get out of the way, as you will most likely do if you make the wrong choice.

EXPERIENCES BUILD DEFENDABLE MARKET LEADERSHIP

Many companies are worried about market leadership; customer experience provides a unique platform for that leadership—leadership through customer commitment and loyalty. The value of the customer should be presented as defendable market leadership. Members of the press and analysts who are accustomed to the traditional measures will be amazed to see a different model that delivers higher and longer lasting returns per customer.

Lower customer churn and higher referrals will be other factors to demonstrate the value increase in the company.

When Mark Benioff launched his company Salesforce.com,[1] it was a rule-changing move. While the rest of the industry sold sales automation software, he offered it as a service at a minimum charge of $65 per person per month. It was a brand new business model that changed the rules in the market. Benioff knew that changing the rules is not a matter of press announcements; instead, he launched a complete communication campaign, based in large part on guerrilla marketing, such as picketing the user conferences of his competitors and handing out *No Software* buttons to users.

His relentless efforts paid off, not only by growing business at Salesforce.com and recruiting Fortune 500 customers to his customer base, but also by forcing his largest competitor, Siebel, to launch a similar service with IBM. Today software as a service is a common option in the industry, but Benioff built a defendable position that led the company into a successful IPO in June 2004. Changing the rules paid off. It caught the competition off guard and unready and allowed Salesforce.com to build their business while others were scrambling to understand what was going on and how they were doing it.

Customer experiences are about creating a unique and easily defendable market position that will make you the envy of every other industry competitor. It will bring you back to the leadership position you were craving. It's just that it will be leadership as defined by your most important stakeholder (if you made the right choice): the customer.

EMPLOYEES EXPERIENCES: THE CUSTOMER EXPERIENCE ENABLERS

As you are approaching the formation of your strategy, do not make the typical mistake of focusing on only half of your challenge (the customers). In today's ever-increasing commoditization of products and services, your employees are also a competitive advantage. They are the ones that stamp the experience with a personal and human touch that forges a strong commitment and relationship.

Forgetting the employee experience is starting the strategy out on the wrong foot. As Southwest Airlines likes to say, "Our customers are not number one." Employees are number one; the customers come second. Your employees are the key to your growth through innovation and to longer and more profitable relationships with customers.

Design and implement an amazing experience that makes your employees want to give you their best and more. How would you know if you got there? Look at the ratio of applicants to each job you post. The stronger your employee experiences, the larger the number of applicants per job posting. The word will travel fast and you will be able to attract the type of talent you have been seeking.

The basis of an amazing employee experience is not money. It is a mission. It is a commitment to make a difference. If all companies would live up to their marketing slogans, the world would look completely different. The problem is that most of the inspiring slogans, describing inspirational commitments, face a crushing reality internally, so they are quickly destroyed by the well-oiled machine of corporate cynicism. Change these machines. Change the crushing reality and you have the key to success.

To achieve this change you will have to make a tough choice that puts people above technology or efficiency. You will have to recognize and design your business to reflect this conviction and utilize your most important assets, your people. The key to success is not declarations. It is operational planning and execution. Your employees will judge you by what you do, not what you say. At the end of the day, the path to profitability, revenues, and effectiveness goes through the customer experience. The path to customer experience excellence goes through the employee experience.

THE NEVER-ENDING DATE

The key to success in personal relationships is never to take the other person for granted—never to settle, but to keep on surprising them and demonstrating your renewed commitment. Most relationships go through their ups and downs, but those that survive are the ones built on the understanding that the dating game is never over. Marriage does not represent the end, but the beginning. Commitment does not imply that the courting is over. If anything, the courting must move into higher gear. Partners need reassurances that they made the right choice. They need to be reminded that despite what is out there, they are in the right relationship with the right partner. Stronger commitments and relationships usually require greater efforts to retain them.

The same line of thinking applies in business. The sale should never be over. Companies should never assume that the customer is "acquired" or in their pocket. The mentality of customers as a destination must be replaced with one that sees the customer as a journey. This requires planning and an understanding of what we want this relationship to produce for each partner two to three years from now. It requires a road map beyond the first sale.

When companies restrict their warranties and guarantees to short periods, they usually behave as if the sale is over and they are moving on to the next customer. They act as if marriage is the endgame, not the beginning. They clearly send a message to the customer regarding their expectations from the relationship: short, quick, and profitable, and then you are on your own.

Smart companies design a mechanism in which the sale is never over. They do not abandon their products the moment the customer signs the credit card slip. Their products are not orphans in the hands of unfamiliar parents. They retain ownership and responsibility for their products, and they make sure the customer is taken care of. They do so because it makes sense financially. If their products are in the hands of the right customers, meaning they made the right choice of customers, then most likely any support they provide will lead to additional business. This is something that they already planned as part of a longer relationship with the customer. By taking responsibility beyond the sale and assuming responsibility when things go wrong, companies are extending their experiences with customers. By extending the experience beyond the moment of the sale, they extend their relationships and potential business.

Smart companies view sales not as an event to be recorded for the next quarterly results, but as a starting point of the relationship. Their actions after the sale is complete are even more critical, as the customers will need assurances that they made the right choice. The initial commitment they provided during the purchase is in contrast to all the other options they have considered but did not purchase. The post-sales experience and customer dialogue are all geared to provide reassurances and make customers comfortable with their choices. When they feel this comfort, they are more ready to act on the role you have designed for them, such as recommending, providing referrals, upgrading, or providing insight.

Customer-centric companies realize that the courtship period is never over. In fact, it is intensified after the first sale. You now need to make good on all those promises you made, in order to establish a relationship that lasts beyond the casual one-night stand. Many such companies have recognized that focusing on the customer is not matter of degree but a matter of survival. You cannot be 55% pregnant or 34% in love. You are either in love or not. This is a 100% commitment. This is not just a commitment of one person or department, and this is where many failed. It is not a one-time program. It is a lifestyle. It is about your DNA, which guides your everyday operations and execution. It is the guidance for the thousands of everyday decisions your sales, service, and accounting people (among others) are making every day. Daily, through those decisions, they choose for customers or against them. The choice is yours.

Endnote

1. Steve Hamm, "Who Says CEOs Can't Find Inner Peace?" (New York: *Business Week,* September 1, 2003), p. 77.

APPENDIX

AN OPEN LETTER TO THE SMART CUSTOMER

Dear Customer,

It is time to take stock of your situation. You hate the way you are treated by your suppliers. You cannot remember the last time you had to wait less than 15 minutes on the phone in pursuit of a decent response to your problem. Product quality is declining and you feel trapped, without many options. Everyone is pretty much the same. "Where did all the good products and services go?" you ask yourself. What has happened to great service and exciting products? Why do they all seem like a pale version of the original? It seems as if quality and service are no longer in vogue. Come to think of it, they have been out of fashion for quite some time.

There is a lot of truth in these feelings—but the bad news is that you have done much to exacerbate the situation. Like any other relationship, it takes two to tango. And you, the customer, stopped dancing. Fascinated by everyday low prices, you kept on chasing the last discount dollar and left your suppliers stranded. You pursued the endlessly lower price phenomenon with zeal and excitement, and now you're wondering why the service and quality are not there. You made a choice to implement a price strategy, and now you wonder why your partner in the relationship, that is, the company, did not continue to deliver high quality and amazing service. In many ways, it was you who forced the company to lower quality, because they needed to adhere to your ever lower price expectations. It was a survival mode for them. They had to do it to stay in business. Your discount addiction came with a price. You didn't think you could get a discount without paying a price, did you? The price was delivered to you in lower quality, smaller quantity, nonexistent caring, and ignorant service. These are all prices that companies have to pay to adapt to your newly found low prices.

In your endless pursuit and support of low prices, you also abandoned your partner. You switched partners on the basis of the lowest common denominator only, price. In such a case, your partner, the company, is paying higher costs just to get your attention each time, again and again. When you were loyal, the company could have lowered their customer attraction costs and applied them to providing more value to you. Now, in the absence of any loyalty, they have to catch your attention every day. This effort has a price. You are, in a sense, paying for your lack of loyalty in lesser value.

Although not all the illnesses of your company–customer relationships are your fault, it is important for you to realize that you own part of the responsibility. The decline in value and quality is destined to continue as long as you take all value for granted and refuse to pay more than the absolute bare minimum for it. For the absolute bare minimum price, you will receive the absolute bare minimum value. It is a simple, natural law of relationships. It is called reciprocity, or as the old adage goes, "You get what you pay for." You really did not think you could cheat the system, did you?

So now what? You have a choice to make. Just like your partner faces some tough choices. To survive and thrive, companies will have to select their customers carefully and weed out the discount addicts. The discount addicts are destined to receive ever-declining value to match their unstoppable appetite for lower prices. They will continue to believe that they cheat the system, but in fact, they will continue to receive lesser value.

Your choice is this: what kind of customer do you want to be? You may shop for value or for price. But you cannot do both at the same time. (And I do not care what all these discount stores are promising you.) You cannot continue dancing on all possible stages if you seek value and excellence from your suppliers. If you want innovation, quality, exciting products, great, committed service, and amazing experiences, you will have to pay the price. If you are willing to give up these factors, then go for the price and keep on shopping for the cheapest products regardless of the brands. When you do so, do not forget to lower your expectations and do not get upset when you are on hold for 25 minutes and then answered by an ignorant person. It is what you chose.

Smart customers will make a serious choice. They will choose which products and services are important to them and which are not, which products are high value and which ones are of no value. For the high-value products, they will kick their discount addiction (I know it is hard, like kicking any other addiction—and for some it is a sin to buy retail). They will forge a real, lasting bond with the supplying company. They will stay on board long enough to build lasting relationships with the company and justify the company's investment in them. Despite the temptations, they will fight the urge and they will not defect the first time they see a lower advertised price in the local outlet and closeouts store. They will save the trips to those stores for the no-value products they do not care about; the products and services for which they are willing to accept lower value and quality; and the products for which they are willing to lower their expectations.

For each customer, the balance between the high-value and no-value products may be different. But the choice needs to be made. One cannot continue to apply high expectations, high-value thinking to no-value pricing. This is the cause of many of your frustrations today.

For customers who are seeking high value, and are willing to pay for it, this will be a time to start taking a stronger stance. Coming from a position of strength, paying higher prices, staying longer, repeating business, these customers will have a stronger claim to their partnering company. They will have to begin to take a more active role in the products and services future. They will not be able to ignore every request for insight, but rather will become active participants in the product's destiny.

Needless to say, strong, lasting relationships will not be justified if the companies are not willing to reciprocate. So customers will have to select their partners carefully. But companies, for their part, are tired of the never-ending discount game. They are seeking true partners whom they can service with value-adding, innovative products and not just paler versions of the originals.

The time has come to form a different relationship. It is time to shed the wishful thinking and be realistic. Either adapt your expectations or your price point. Every relationship must be profitable to the providing company or it will go out of business. No one but you will pay for your products' value. So you ought to make the choice—either you are ready for a real relationship or you want to continue the discount addiction. You, too, have a choice to make.

P.S. Relationships are all about reciprocity. If you care for service with a smile, think about smiling first. Spread a smile, and you will significantly increase your chances of getting one in return. It is a business of people. Do your share and, miraculously, others will reciprocate.

INDEX